MW01680667

CHARMING
SMALL HOTEL
GUIDES

Southern France

CHARMING
SMALL HOTEL
GUIDES

Southern France

Edited by Jenny Rees

DUNCAN PETERSEN

HUNTER
PUBLISHING INC

300 Raritan Center Parkway,
CN 94, Edison, N.J. 08818

Copyright © Jenny Rees
© Duncan Petersen Publishing Ltd 1997

All rights reserved. No reproduction, copy or transmission of this publication may be made without written permission. No paragraph of this publication may be reproduced, copied or transmitted save with written permission or in accordance with the provisions of the Copyright Act 1956 (as amended). Any person who does any unauthorized act in relation to this publication may be liable to criminal prosecution and civil claims for damages.

Conceived, designed and produced by
Duncan Petersen Publishing Ltd

Editor	Jenny Rees
Inspectors	Matthew Hayes, Suzanne Kelleher Peter Henson, Nicola Swallow
Art director	Mel Petersen
Maps	Christopher Foley

This edition published in the UK and Commonwealth 1997 by
Duncan Petersen Publishing Ltd,
31 Ceylon Road, London W14 OYP.

Sales representation in the UK and Ireland by
World Leisure Marketing,
9 Downing Road, West Meadows Industrial Estate,
Derby DE21 6HA.

Distributed by
Grantham Book Services

ISBN 1 872576 63 X

A CIP catalogue record for this book is available
from the British Library

AND

Published in the USA 1997 by
Hunter Publishing Inc.,
300 Raritan Center Parkway, CN 94, Edison, N.J. 08818.
Tel (908) 225 1900 Fax (908) 417 0482

ISBN 1-55650-783-6

Typeset by Duncan Petersen Publishing Ltd
Originated by Reprocolor International S.R.I., Milan
Printed by G. Z. Printek, S.A.L., Bilbao

Contents

Introduction

This is the twelfth title in the now well-established series of *Charming Small Hotel Guides* and – for the second time – we look at a region rather than a whole country.

Enthusiasts of the series will be familiar with the all-France guide and will recognize in these pages certain hotels that have become favourites of ours over the years. These we felt we could not, fairly, ignore. *But* this guide is far from being a duplicate of the all-France book: it looks at the area in more depth, as you would expect given more space. We have gathered into this new guide a wide selection of new discoveries: previously uninspected hotels that will now, we feel sure, also become favourites, for they have the necessary qualities. And we have filled in some gaps of which we were aware in the all-France guide.

Occasionally an unforeseen event governs our selection of hotels. One of the stalwarts of our all-France guide, the Mas d'Aigret, at Les Baux-de-Provence, was deserted and looking sadly neglected at the time of our inspection. It had, we learned from owners Pip Phillips and his wife, Chantal, been temporarily closed down because of rocks falling from a crag of the Alpilles, the beautiful range of mini-mountains in that part of Provence. This natural upset could not have come at a worse time: the Mas d'Aigret had just been voted Number One Hotel/Restaurant in France by customers of VFB, the British specialist agents for holidays in France, and awarded two *toques* by Gault-Millau for outstanding cuisine. We look forward to news of the re-opening of the hotel.

Ground covered

This guide covers the territory south of an imaginary line between Bordeaux and Geneva. In many people's minds 'the South of France' is the coastal area known as the Côte d'Azur, plus associated parts of Provence. Here we cover not only Provence and the Côte d'Azur but a *much* larger area, which is why, to make the distinction, we have entitled the guide *Southern France.*

Within Southern France we have made our own seven 'regions' out of groups of *départements* – the 'counties' into which France is so neatly divided, each with its own identifying postal code which is attached to every address. Our regions do not correspond in any way to the official administrative regions, for our lines have been drawn with the intention of being helpful to the traveller by proposing manageable areas to visit. Maps of each of the seven regions are on pages 19-31, with accompanying text describing their character.

We know that many travellers use the *Charming Small Hotel Guides* as key reference material for planning motoring tours and we have kept such travellers particularly in mind when drawing up the seven regions: Bordeaux and the Dordogne; the South-West; Languedoc-Roussillon; Auvergne and the Massif Central; Provence-Côte d'Azur; Rhône Valley; and the Alps.

Introduction

Southern France

People the world over, but particularly those condemned to live in the grey climate of Northern Europe, have long thought of the Mediterranean south as Heaven on Earth: a sun-blessed landscape of olive groves and vineyards, with cornflower skies and deep-blue sea, an abundance of wine, fruit that can be picked off the tree or found heaped in baskets in village market squares, and a carefree way of life. More recently, it has been seen as the perfect antidote to the pressure of city life.

Sadly, however, the more people have sought escape on the shores of the Mediterranean, the more they have spoiled what they seek to find. It is not surprising then that many visitors prefer instead the relatively undeveloped hinterland behind the coast. This new collection of hotels reflects that significant shift. 'Green' tourism, too, is gathering momentum; don't lock up your chickens any longer if you are a hotelier looking for success.

Not everyone, as we know, will be heading for the coast. There are now many other well-defined regions of Southern France that are fast catching up on Provence and the Côte d'Azur: the Dordogne, with its rivers and verdant countryside; the wilder Auvergne; the Alps, with their ever-increasing number of summer visitors. Peace and quiet and privacy have become much sought-after elements of a holiday and hoteliers are very aware of this demand. Comfort – and even luxury – is also, with today's affluence, considered by some to be an essential ingredient of the kind of holiday that one would like to remember forever. The face of French hotel-keeping has changed much to cater for an evolving clientele. We've taken note of these changes.

Charming and small

There really are relatively few *genuine* charming small hotels. Unlike other guides, we are particularly fussy about size, rarely straying over 15 bedrooms. If a hotel has more than that, it needs to have the *feel* of a much smaller place to be in this guide.

We attach more importance to size than other guides because we think that unless a hotel is small, it cannot give a genuinely personal welcome, or make you feel like an individual, rather than just a guest. For what we mean by a personal welcome, read on.

Unlike other guides, we often rule out places that have great qualities, but are nonetheless no more nor less than – hotels. Our hotels are all special in some way.

We think that we have a much clearer idea than other guides of what is special and what is not; and we think we apply these criteria more consistently than other guides because we are a small and personally managed company rather than a bureaucracy. We have a small team of like-minded inspectors, chosen by the editor and thoroughly rehearsed in recognizing what we want. While we very much appreciate readers' reports – see below – they are not our main source of information.

Last but by no means least, we're independent – there's no payment for inclusion.

So what exactly do we look for?

* An attractive, preferably peaceful setting.

* A building that is either handsome or interesting or historic, or at least with a distinct character.

* Ideally, we look for adequate space, but on a human scale: we don't go for places that rely on grandeur, or that have pretensions that could intimidate.

* Decoration must be harmonious and in good taste, and the furnishings and facilities comfortable and well maintained. We like to see interesting antique furniture that is there because it can be used, not simply revered. Although we list trouser presses, we only do so as an indication of the level of comfort.

* The proprietors and staff need to be dedicated and thoughtful, offering a personal welcome, *without being intrusive.* The guest needs to feel like an individual.

Whole-page entries

We rarely see all of these qualities together in place; but our warmest recommendations – whole page, with photograph – usually combine all but one or two of these qualities.

Half-page entries

Don't, however, ignore our half-page entries. They are very useful addresses: *all* are *genuine* charming small hotels, by no means just space-fillers. You can't have stars on every page.

French hotels, past and present

The small French hotel of the past has moved on, though there remain scattered examples – and very charming they are – of the almost caricature model of what could be found about 100 years ago: front door off the street or village square, little restaurant on the ground floor, where locals come in for a *petit café* in the morning and a drink at lunchtime, dark winding stairs up to a landing, bedrooms with deer racing across the wallpaper,

No fear, no favour

This is an independent guide. The selection has been made after thorough research, personal recommendation and expert assessment by the editor and a small team of helpers. **No establishment pays to be in this guide.**

infuriating lighting, and a shower and bidet boxed into a corner of the room, with very thin walls. Odd noises could be heard through the night.

Le patron would be at the bar, while Mme, often on the short-tempered side, occupied herself with guests. Although deeply conservative in many ways, the French pride themselves on their ability to move with the times and be *à la mode.* Today some of those same hotel families now offer air-conditioning and whirlpool or spa baths, while at the same time retaining an old-fashioned charm and natural hospitality that draws visitors from all over the world and every year finds a new following.

In our assessment of this collection of establishments in Southern France we have, we hope, identified a wide range of different types of charm. Sometimes you may have to wait until the end of the day for the charm of the view from the terrace at the setting of the sun. In some hotels, the aesthetic pleasure given by the interior decoration and furnishings provides the charm. In others, the building itself, or its garden, will be charming. Sometimes there will be someone in charge – maybe an entire family – who radiate charm and may, in some instances, make up for deficiencies elsewhere. Then there are the very special cases where the whole *ensemble* is charming – or the charm is quite simply in the spirit of the place.

Charming Small Hotels have made their mark not only because of the places they feature, but also for the way in which they are edited, designed and produced. Our entries employ, above all, words; they contain not one symbol. They are written by people who have something to say and not by a faceless bureaucracy which has long since lost the ability to distinguish the praiseworthy from the mediocre.

Every entry aims to give a definite feel of what it is actually like to stay in that place. The editorial team is small and highly experienced at assessing hotels, and at noticing all-important details. Although we place great emphasis on consistency, we make use in these guides of reports from readers and urge you to tell us what you think of the places you visit. (See page 32.)

We have not excluded hotels from the guide just because they are expensive.

We know, of course, that the majority of our readers will not be millionaires nor indeed back-packers, travelling on a shoestring. The majority lie somewhere between the two extremes. We include some expensive hotels because they are special – and charming – and can be used as the once-in-a-lifetime treat or indulgence of the holiday or visit. Expense, however, may well mean that the hotel gets a short entry rather than a long one.

The full-page entries with colour photographs are our warmest recommendations – the stars, as it were, of our collection – BUT the short entries (four to a page) on pages 145 to 181 are equally charming and could be described as the all-important supporting cast.

Our selection, as usual, covers a wide range of places, for all pockets and all tastes – Relais & Châteaux hotels; four-star hotels; city, town, village, country, resort hotels; *auberges*; restaurants-with-rooms and *chambres d'hôtes*.

When in France...

Hotel-keeping is a respected profession in France at all levels. Many small hotels are family-run and have been for generations. There are times when these establishments are very busy, when all the resources of a limited staff are being pushed to the limit and these are not times to make unnecessary demands on the management. The French enjoy and cherish their social formalities and can become very agitated if unable to conform to them.

As a basic rule, for example, it is asking for trouble to turn up at a hotel around noon, and expect instant service at reception, for this is when lunch is beginning. The French are famous for taking food seriously and eat early. If you want to have a pleasant meal, it is dangerous to leave going into the restaurant for lunch much after noon and by 1 pm you may well be turned away. Dinner can be served as early as 7 pm, particularly in country areas; hotels will expect you to be having an aperitif any time from 6 pm. Hoteliers will not be distracted from what they consider to be their crucial duty – getting meals to the table – and at these times visitors can find themselves in potentially embarrassing and even explosive situations if they present themselves at the reception desk asking unwelcome questions. This is how many misunderstandings arise. It is not that anyone wishes to be unpleasant. If faced with obstruction to what is considered to be the main business of the day, hotel owners or staff feel angry and frustrated because they cannot give their restaurant customers the service they deserve, and also because they cannot give proper service at the reception desk.

The afternoon can also be sensitive. This is when it appears that all useful people in the hotel disappear and the place seems deserted. This is not a good time to turn up and expect to be cordially received, either.

We have found on our travels that in many hotels, even those towards the coast, the social formality ethic also extends to dress. This is not an easy one, for it is really an understanding, not a written rule (though in some cases it is). Unless eating by the pool, guests are expected to dress correctly at meals and in the public rooms of the hotel: that is, not in swimming costumes or sunbathing attire. Towelling robes are often provided in the rooms precisely for the purpose of covering up *en route* for the pool. In the Vaucluse, one of our inspectors witnessed a group of scantily-clad guests fooling around on the stairs of a hotel in a listed historic building. (They were sent packing.)

Some hotels ask their guests to 'dress' for dinner; this does not mean long skirts or black ties, but is a request to wear something befitting a meal (which may be candle-lit) that has been prepared with great care by the chef and served in a manner worthy of it.

Chambres d'hôtes

Chambres d'hôtes, originally conceived in France as a way of giving town and city people a chance to stay in the country in simple, reasonably-priced accommodation, have become much more sophisticated of late. More and more professional people – of all nationalities – are choosing to open up their own houses – often beautifully decorated and furnished with treasured personal possessions, to paying guests. Staying in a *chambre d'hôte* can be a most interesting and rewarding experience, but it is not, in any way, like staying in an hotel. Guests do not have the same freedom as in an hotel or the same right to expect a certain standard of service (even though they may sometimes be paying more). Always bear in mind that you are a guest in a private house. Do not arrive without booking; telephone if you have been held up and are going to be late.

Children

It is a popularly held belief that the French love their children. They do – but not always in hotels. We always ask the question 'Do you accept children?'; the answer is generally 'Of course'. But not, by any means, in every case. Many quite understandable, reasons are given for not accepting them: our hotel is filled with treasured family furniture, fragile *objets* and porcelain; we have many regular guests who come for the peace and quiet we offer here; silence is golden; many of our guests are of a certain age; many of our guests have come to escape from their children. Some hotels specify that they accept 'well-behaved' children. To avoid disappointment or a difficult situation, be quite sure how the hotel feels about children before booking.

Pets

We ask whether hotels accept pets and, in a country that now owns more cats and dogs even than Britain, the answer is normally in the affirmative. Often one of the most entertaining moments in the daily life of a French hotel is the after-dinner ritual of walking the dog: one's fellow guests take on a different guise when heard whistling and calling to their pets through the darkness in the grounds.

But hotels have a wide variety of rules relating to pets. Some allow dogs in the restaurant, some don't. Some prefer dogs to stay in rooms for as much of the day as possible; some would rather dogs stay in rooms for as little of the day as possible and never alone, because of scratching damage to doors and furnishings. Some establishments will only take cats. In general, dogs are not allowed anywhere near swimming-pools – in particular, large dogs with a liking for water.

Air-conditioning
Air-conditioning is by no means common in French hotels, but little by little it is being introduced. Air-conditioners make a noise and do not work effectively if the windows are open. It is, nevertheless, a boon in very hot weather, because it helps to give a good night's sleep. It is well worth finding a hotel with air-conditioning – if only for one night – when driving south in the summer months; after a long, tiring day in the car and the prospect of another day's driving in the heat, the benefits of a restful night will make paying the bill considerably less painful.

Historic houses
Historic houses have histories and are old. The better the renovation work, the more likely it is that some of the bedrooms may not resemble what is expected. It may sound like fun to stay in a converted abbey, but a week in a windowless monks' cell could turn out to be a little grim. Be very sure what you are getting when you book. In the busy high season, there is little chance of moving rooms after arriving.

The same principle applies to bathrooms. Although we have paid careful attention to bathrooms in our inspections, some less-than-perfect ones are bound to have slipped through our net. Bathrooms in towers, for example, may sometimes not be as quite as romantic as they sound.

Breakfast
Generally, breakfast in a French hotel will consist of coffee (or tea), a basket of bread, rolls, croissants and, perhaps, *brioche,* jam (often home-made) and some butter. But – and mostly you aren't told this – there are usually a number of alternatives, such as eggs (boiled, scrambled, fried), fruit and, in some places (normally with non-French owners), ham, bacon or cheese. Always ask what is available. French breakfasts are now reaching record-breaking prices – a small survey we conducted found that 100 francs is not unusual.

How to find an entry
The guide is divided into seven geographical regions (see the maps, pages 19-31) but within that the arrangement is alphabetical, by village or town or city.

The 112 full-page entries are on pages 33-144, organized as described above – first regionally, and within each regional section alphabetically.

The shorter entries are on pages 145-181, arranged in the same way.

To find a hotel in a particular area, look through the headings at the top of the pages until you find that area – or use the maps, pages 19-31, which show the place name and number of the page on which that hotel is described.

Introduction

To locate a specific hotel in a specific place, use the indexes at the back of the book. One index lists the hotels by their names; the other by location.

How to read an entry
At the top of each entry is a **coloured bar** giving the name of the town or village where the establishment is found, along with a categorization which gives some clue to its character. Then follows the description.

At the foot of the description is the **fact box** containing facts and figures that should help you to decide if the hotel is in your price range and has the facilities you want.

Address
First of these facts is the **address**, which, in some cases, might be in remote countryside or in a small village or hamlet. A detailed map is always useful: we recommend the *Michelin Motoring Atlas of France* or the IGN (Institut Géographique National) regional tourist maps.

Tel
Under **tel** we give the telephone numbers. All telephone numbers in France were changed in October 1996: the old eight-figure numbers were replaced by ten-figure numbers, old numbers being prefixed by a two-digit area code. In this guide, the new area codes are 04 for South-East France and 05 for South-West France. (To dial from Paris to the provinces and from the provinces to Paris, use the new ten-figure number.)

Fax
We are able to give a **fax** number for the majority of our recommended hotels, but there are still a few places that – for a variety of reasons – refuse to have a fax machine. One hotelier told us that it is too easy to make a booking by fax – in a large number of cases his would-be clients just never turned up – and his time was wasted when he had a machine. Another hotelier, who had created a beautifully simple and quiet place, said he didn't approve of modern fads and whatever was the matter with the phone and the mail, anyway. On the whole, though, hoteliers are good at swift replies to inquiries by fax.

Car Parking
We were impressed, on our travels for this guide, with the concern shown by hoteliers for the safety of guests' cars – large numbers of Mercedes were being stolen from hotel car parks at that time and there were outbreaks of vandalism, particularly in the more popular parts of Provence and the Côte d'Azur. One hotelier told of the morning he awoke to find all the cars in his car park had been broken into; that same day he ordered a high

wire mesh fence and a security gate. Where we mention 'secure parking', we mean that there are gates that are closed at night – or indeed during the day – or an infra-red alarm system.

Prices

Where available, we have provided a range of **prices** from the cheapest single room in low season to the most expensive double in high season, though many hotels do not differentiate between seasons. In France, you pay per room (usually a double room), not per person, but there are a few exceptions to this practice, particularly in the skiing resorts. Generally, breakfast is not included in the price of the room, though, again, there rare exceptions. To give an idea of how much the bill might come to for one night, we have included the price of breakfast.
Always check on prices when booking; we have been as accurate as possible, but hotels do change their prices, particularly if up-grading has taken place.

up to 500FF	F
between 500FF and 800FF	FF
between 800FF and 1,100FF	FFF
more than 1,100FF	FFFF
well over 1,100FF	FFFF+

Credit cards

We use the following abbreviations for **credit cards:**

AE	American Express
DC	Diners Card
EC	Eurocard
MC	MasterCard
V	Visa/Barclaycard/Bank Americard/Carte Bleue

The least often accepted credit cards – particularly in smaller establishments – are American Express and Diners Card.

Useful information

Public holidays in France

January 1st
Easter Day
Easter Monday
Labour Day, May 1st
VE Day, May 8th
Whit Monday
Bastille Day, July 14th
Assumption Day, August 15th
All Saints Day, November 1st
Remembrance Day, November 11th
Christmas Day, December 25th

Information centres
All over France, there are 5,000 *Offices de Tourism* and *Syndicats d'Initiative*, which give advice on accommodation, restaurants, hotels and local transport.

Motoring in France

Drinking and driving
It is not wise to drink and drive in France, where the limit is 0.05 per cent alcohol and random breath tests are frequent. There are stiff penalties: fines for exceeding the alcohol limit start at 900F (for a rate between 0.05 and 0.08 per cent) and go up to as much as 30,000F.

Police are authorized to impose and collect on-the-spot fines of up to 2,500F from drivers who violate traffic regulations. For minor infractions, other than parking violations, a 30 per cent reduction of the amount of the fine may be granted to drivers who pay immediately or within 24 hours. If the motorist considers he is not at fault, he will be asked to pay a deposit (*amende forfaitaire*) which varies according to the offence (eg 150F for not wearing a seatbelt). Police are required to issue a receipt showing the amount paid.

Speeding fines
Fines may be imposed – from a minimum of 900F (reduced to 600F if payment is made on the spot) to a maximum of 5,000F – for exceeding the speed limit by 30 to 40 kilometres an hour. A new category of offence has been created in the penal code for drivers who 'deliberately put the lives of others in danger'. This applies when a third person has been put in direct danger of injury or death through the driver's disregard for safety precautions (there is a 100,000F fine for causing slight injuries).

These figures are based on the most recently-available information at time of going to press and are liable to change.

Points to remember
* In built-up areas, the *priorité à droite* still applies: you must give way to anybody coming out of a side-turning on the right. However, the *priorité* rule no longer applies at roundabouts, which means you give way to cars already on the roundabout: watch for signs and exercise great caution.
* No driving on a provisional licence.
* Seatbelts must be worn by the driver and front- and back-seat passengers.
* Children under ten may not travel in the front of the car unless sitting in a specially approved fitted seat facing backwards.
* Stop signs mean stop. Creeping slowly in first gear will not do. Come to a complete halt.
* There must be no stopping on open roads unless the car is dri-

ven off the road.
* Overtaking where there is a solid single line is **heavily** penalized.
* Headlight beams must be adjusted for driving on the right-hand side of the road. Yellow-tinted headlights are **not** compulsory for tourist vehicles.
* If a driver flashes his lights in France, he is generally indicating that he has priority and that you should give way.

Motorways

There are more than 8,000 kilometres of motorway in France, mostly toll roads (or *autoroutes à péages*). Prices per kilometre can vary: the toll from Calais to Menton (1,221 kms) is 453F, and from Calais to Montpellier, a similar distance, 366F.

Every two kilometres there is an orange emergency telephone; parking and rest areas are every ten or 20 kilometres. Approximately every 40 kilometres are 24-hour petrol stations, which offer a basic maintenance service. Most credit cards are accepted as payment for tolls and at service stations.

The charge for assistance on motorways is fixed by the French government and, according to the most recent available figures, rates are 345F for vehicles of up to 1.8 tonnes and 435F for vehicles of between 1.8 tonnes and 3.5 tonnes (plus 45F on Alpine motorways). This covers the cost of repairing the vehicle on the spot (up to 30 minutes) or of towing it up to 5 km beyond the next motorway exit. A 25 per cent supplement is added for assistance at night (from 6 pm to 8 am) and at weekends.

Motorists may only call the police or the official breakdown service operating in that area, and cannot request help from their own assistance company if they break down on a motorway. The same applies on the Paris *périphérique.*

Speed limits

Unless otherwise posted and on dry roads:
* 130 km/h on toll motorways.
* 110 km/h on dual carriageways and non-toll motorways.
* 90 km/h on other roads.
* 50 km/h in towns. The limit begins where you see the roadside sign giving the name of the town and ends where you see a bar through the roadside sign.

On wet roads:
* 110 km/h on toll motorways.
* 100 km/h on dual carriageways and non-toll motorways.
* 80 km/h on other roads.
* There is a new speed limit of 50 km/h on motorways in foggy conditions, when visability is less than 50 metres.

Hotel bookings

When booking you will be asked for a deposit *(arrhes)* equal to

25 per cent of the bill. If you cancel you lose your deposit. If the owner or hotelier cancels, he must pay you double the amount of deposit paid. If you are asked for payment on account *(acompte)*, you are more firmly committed: if you cancel you are liable for payment for the whole stay. Make sure these conditions are absolutely clear before making your booking.

To avoid disappointment, the traveller is advised to book in advance. The most satisfactory way is to do this by fax. Bear in mind that the French often put the month first when writing dates, as in 6.14.97 (14th June, 1997).

Your booked room will normally be kept for you until 6 pm, so it is sensible to telephone if there is a likelihood of arriving at the hotel much after that time.

Payment and credit cards

American Express, Diners Club, MasterCard and Access cards are widely accepted in shops, hotels, restaurants, petrol stations and many hypermarkets for amounts above 80 or 100F. When paying by credit card, check the amount which appears on the receipt: in France no decimal point is shown between *Francs* and *centimes.*

Recently French cards have started to carry personal information, designed to reduce the risk of fraud, in a chip rather than in a magnetic band. If your card is queried because this information can't be read, have your bank's or credit car company's telephone number ready so that you and your card can be verified.

Remember that cards can be used to withdraw cash from machines all over France – of course they need to bear the appropriate symbol.

Service and tips

Service is included in restaurant bills, but you may also wish to leave a tip as a mark of appreciation. It is usual to give porters, doormen, theatre and cinema usherettes, guides, taxi drivers and hairdressers a tip of between 5 and 10F.

Facts about France

* Mont Blanc (4,807 m), in the Savoy Alps, is the highest peak in France, and indeed in Europe.
* Saint-Véran – at 2,200 metres in the Hautes-Alpes – is France's highest- altitude inhabited village.
* There are 6,000 species of plant life – 200 of them specific to France.
* There are 340 different sorts of cheese and about 450 DOC wines.
* The largest beach in Europe (12 km) is at La Baule in the Loire Atlantique *département* of the Western Loire.
* The highest sand dune in France is the Dune du Pilat (150 m) in the Gironde *département* of Aquitaine.

French holiday dates

The French continue to prefer to take their holidays in July and August and take to the roads in their hundreds of thousands, if not millions, at certain times over the summer. If possible, try to avoid travelling on 1st July, the weekend of 14th July, 31st July, 1st August, and the weekend of the 15th August.

With thanks to the French Tourist Office.

Bon voyage.

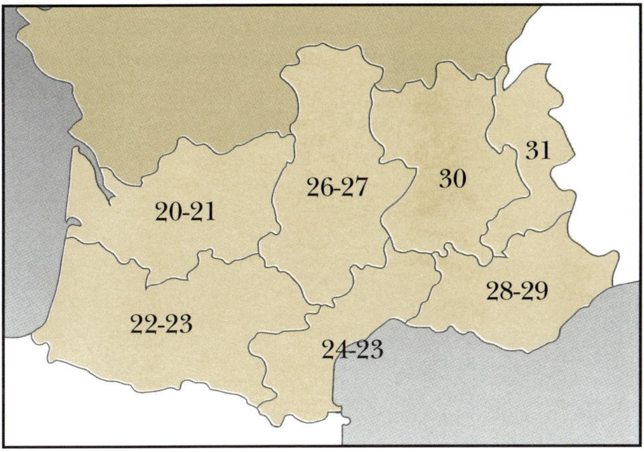

Key to maps of hotel locations and visitor information

Bordeaux and the Dordogne

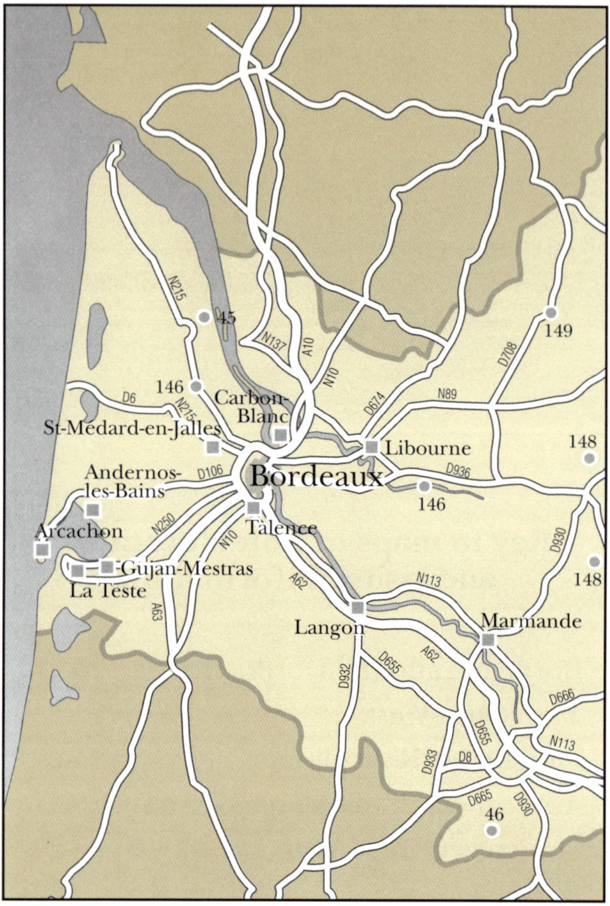

Bordeaux is perhaps one of the best-known parts of France because of the wines that take their names from the villages and châteaux of the famous vineyards. For many travellers it is also the gateway to the green, fertile hinterland generally known as the Dordogne, with pretty pastoral landscapes that seem to have changed little in hundreds of years.

Many of our most charming small hotels are on the winding rivers of the Dordogne and the Lot. With abundant truffles and *foie gras*, the region is a paradise for gourmets.

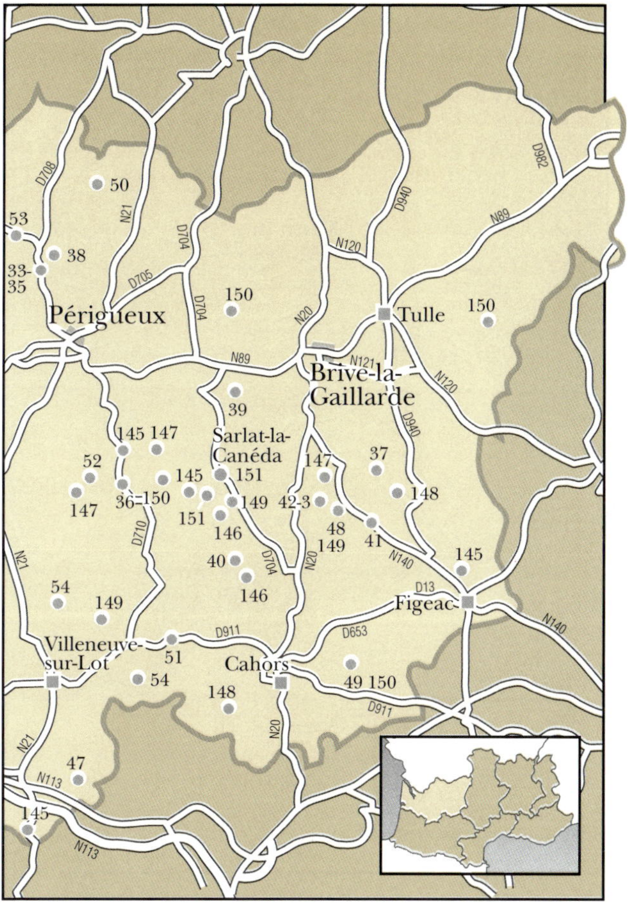
Périgueux
Tulle
Brive-la-Gaillarde
Sarlat-la-Canéda
Figeac
Villeneuve-sur-Lot
Cahors
D708
N21
D704
D705
N20
N120
D940
N89
D982
N121
D710
N140
D13
D911
D653
N113
50
53
38
33-35
150
39
145
147
52
36-150
151
149
42-3
48
41
37
148
146
40
54
51
49
47

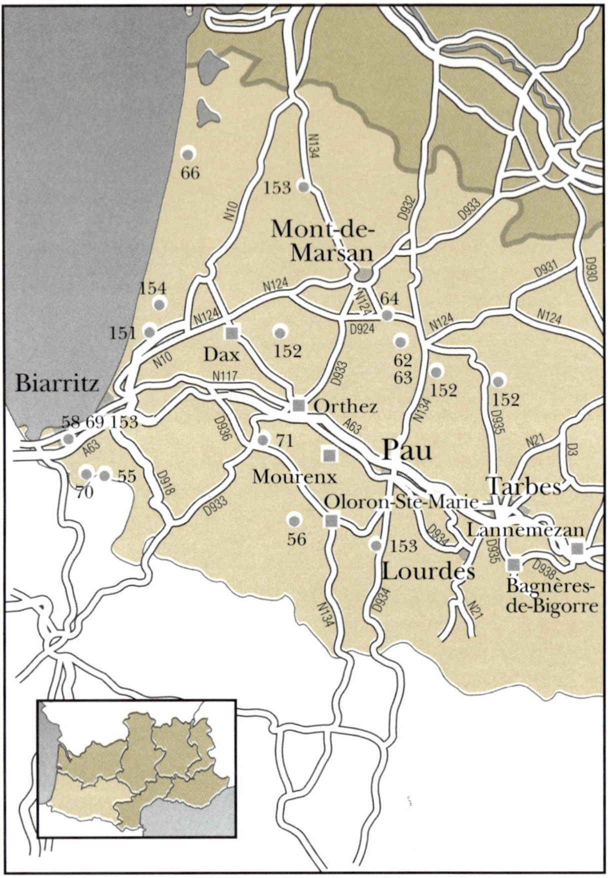

With Atlantic beaches, the strange, immense expanses of the Landes, the Basque country, the Pyrenees and the Spanish border, and fine examples of medieval towns, villages and fortified *bastides*, this is a region rich in diversity, tradition and history. You can also eat memorably – the area is renowned throughout France for its gastronomy and is fiercely proud of its reputation.

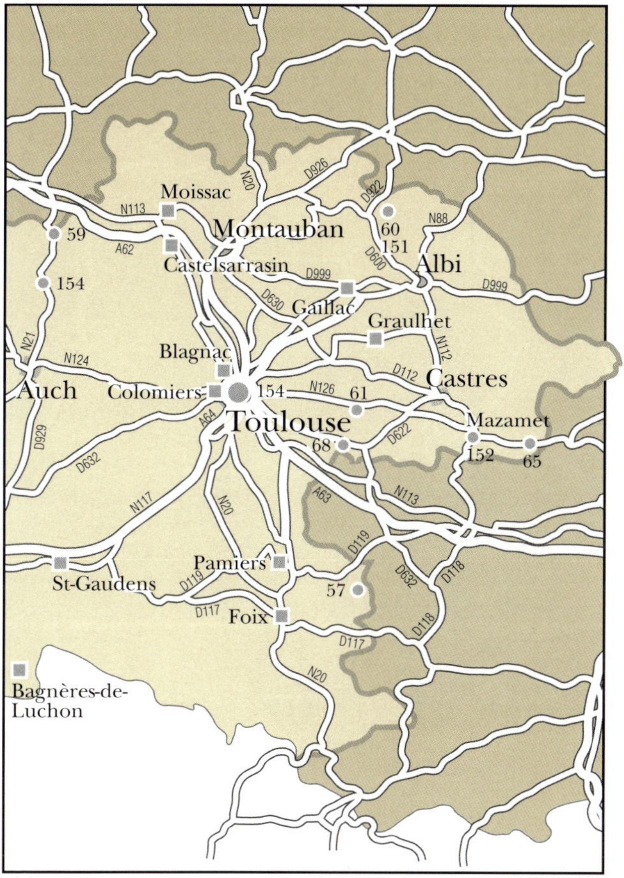
Moissac
N113
59
A62
Montauban
Castelsarrasin
154
N20
D926
D922
60
151
N88
D600
Albi
D999
D999
D630
Gaillac
Graulhet
N112
N21
N124
Blagnac
D112
Castres
Auch
Colomiers
154
N126
61
A64
Toulouse
Mazamet
D929
68
D622
152
65
D632
N113
N117
N20
A63
D119
Pamiers
D632
D118
St-Gaudens
D119
57
D117
Foix
D118
D117
N20
Bagnères-de-
Luchon

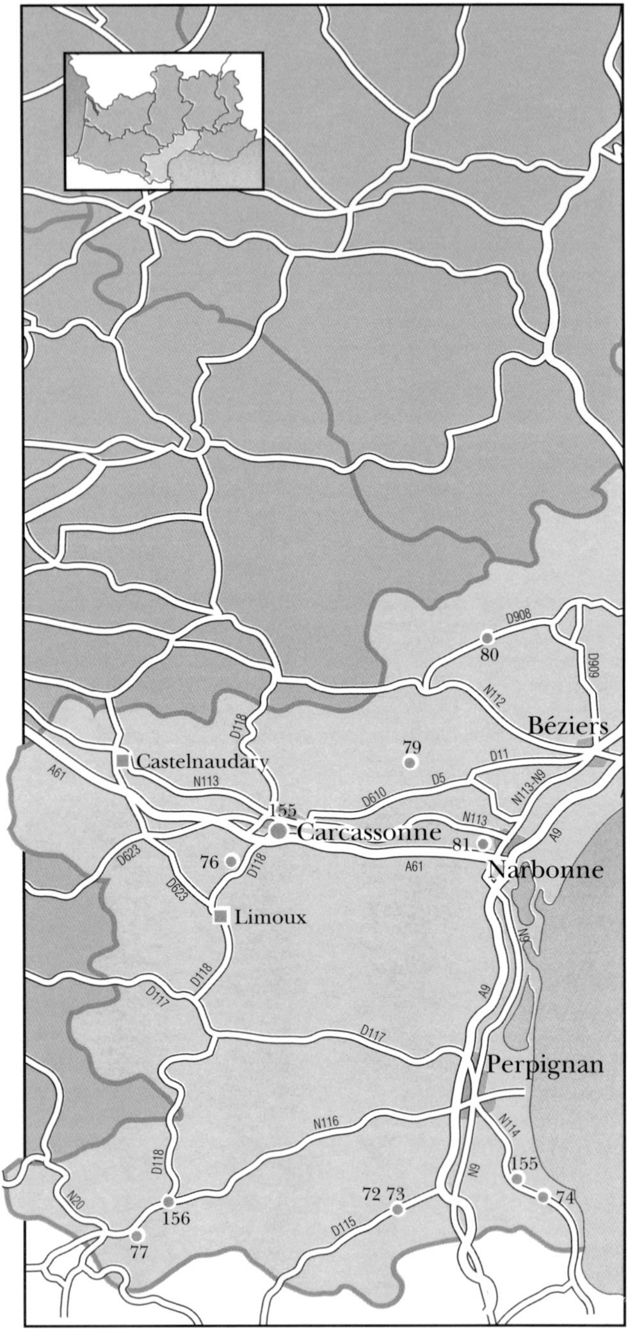
D908
80
D909
N112
Béziers
79
D11
Castelnaudary
A61
N113
D118
D5
D610
N113-N9
155
N113
Carcassonne
81
A9
76
D118
A61
Narbonne
D623
D623
Limoux
N9
D118
A9
D117
D117
Perpignan
N116
N114
D118
155
N9
74
72 73
N20
156
D115
77

Languedoc-Roussillon

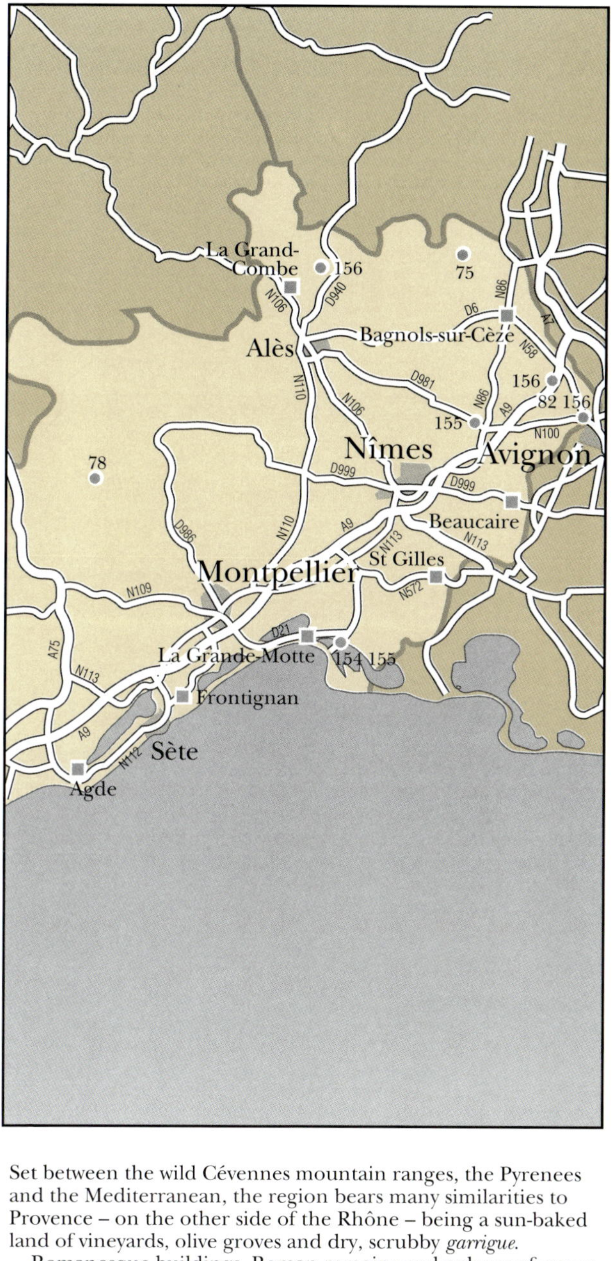

Set between the wild Cévennes mountain ranges, the Pyrenees and the Mediterranean, the region bears many similarities to Provence – on the other side of the Rhône – being a sun-baked land of vineyards, olive groves and dry, scrubby *garrigue.*

Romanesque buildings, Roman remains and palaces of popes and cardinals are among its architectural treasures, and rugby pitches and bullrings are emblems of local passions.

Auvergne and the Massif Central

The Auvergne is at the very heart of France, in the rugged, high Massif Central, with its impressive scenery of mountain ranges, volcanic formations, larva rock, lakes and valleys. Heavily depopulated in the past – many of Paris's bars and cafés are run by *auvergnat* families – the region has been opened up to tourism by modern communications, and ski resorts attract visitors from all over Europe. The area is also well known for cheeses, such as Saint-Nectaire and Auvergne blue.

Auvergne and the Massif Central

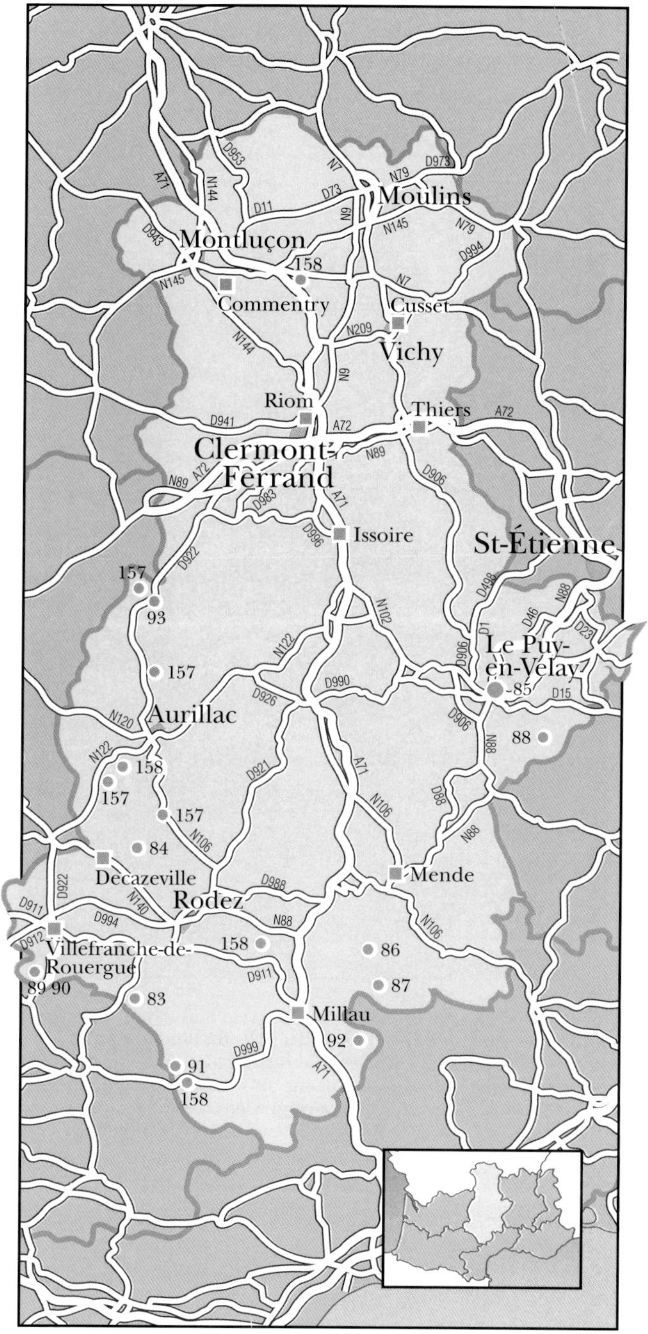

Provence-Côte d'Azur

The allure of Provence – sun, sparkling sea, blue skies, wine, the easy Mediterranean way of life, and a light that has inspired painters through the centuries – continues to work its magic. Not surprisingly, our largest concentration of recommendations is here. Provence is prettiest in spring, when the flowers are at their best, apart from the fields of lavender, which should be seen in midsummer.

Provence-Côte d'Azur

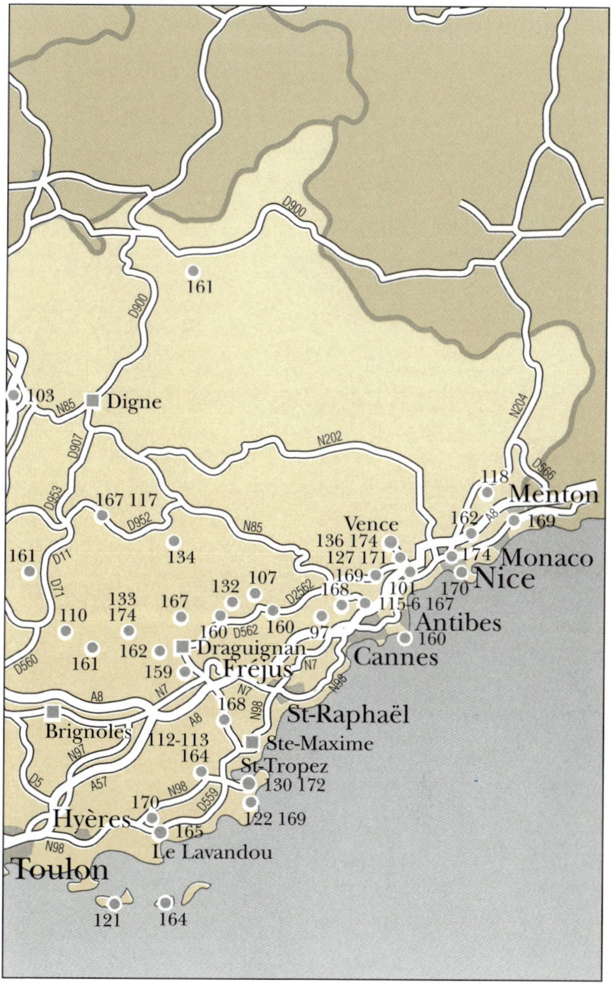

Rhône Valley

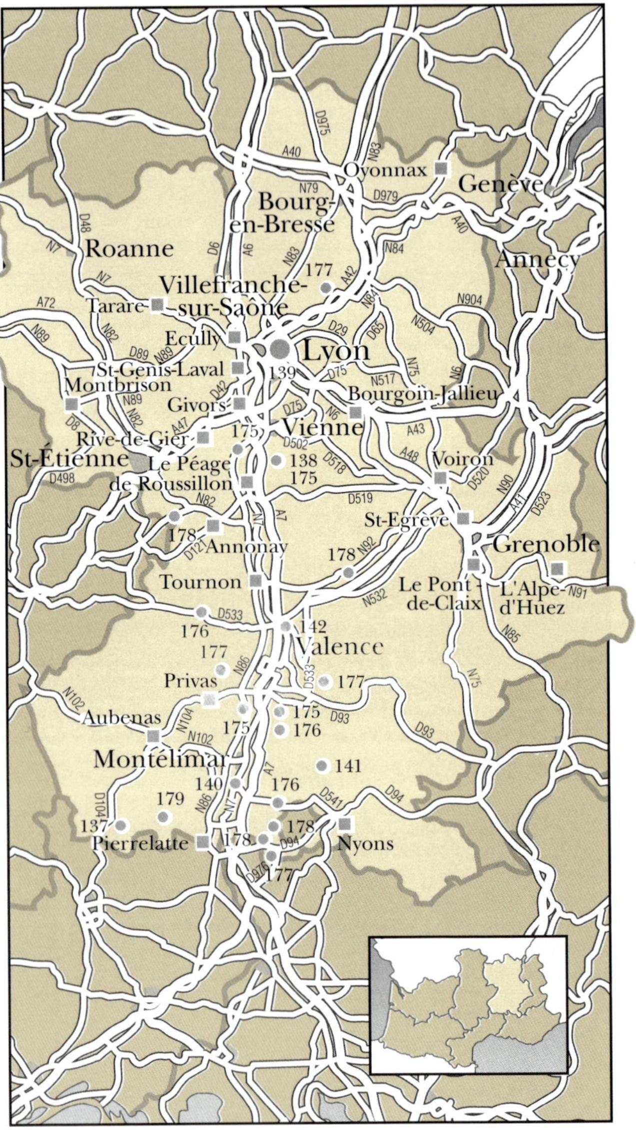

Many visitors see this region only briefly – through the window of a car or a coach – and therefore miss much. Lyon is the gastronomic centre of France, with chefs able to draw on local fish, game, vegetables and fruit, and the wines of the Beaujolais vineyards and the Côtes-du-Rhone villages. The enterprising traveller will want to find time to stop on the route south, to sit under the trees or on a terrace and watch one of the great rivers of Europe go by.

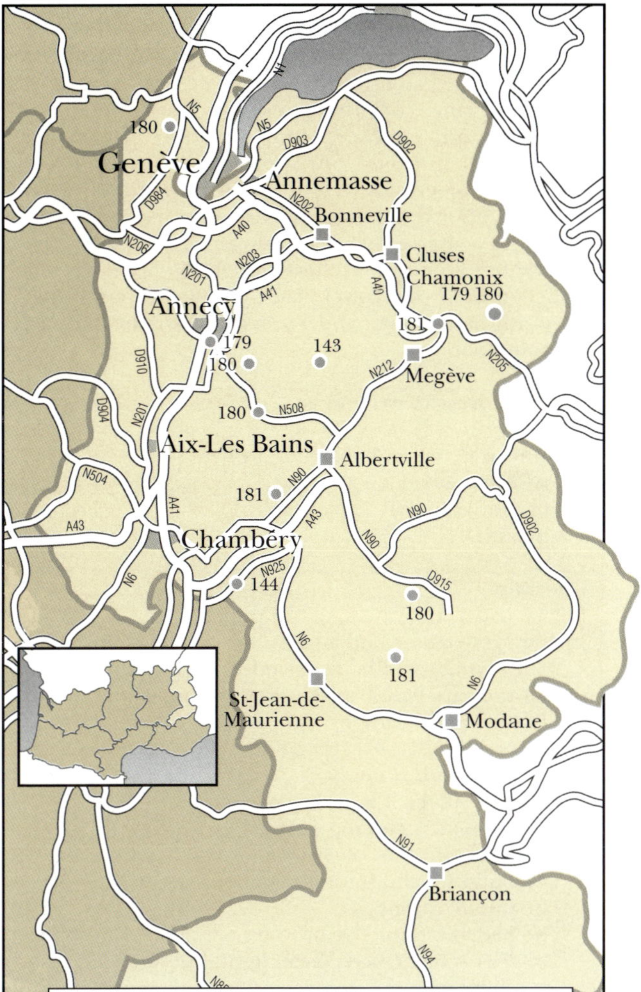

The Alps are not just for skiing: they also offer all kinds of rewards for lovers of nature, walking and wild flowers. June and July are the best months for discovering the great variety of Alpine flora, including gentians, violets and anemones. The French Alpine region stretches from Lake Geneva in the north down to the mountains of Provence, with the highest peak in Europe, Mont Blanc (4,731 metres) in the *département* of Haute-Savoie. Here also is Lake Annecy, much visited by 19thC painters and writers, with pure, clear water, a green shoreline, and a romantic mountain backdrop.

Reporting to the guide

Please write and tell us about your experiences of small hotels, guest-houses and inns, whether good or bad, whether listed in this edition or not. As well as hotels in France, we are interested in hotels in Britain and Ireland, Italy, Spain, Austria, Germany, Switzerland and the USA. We assume that reporters have no objections to our publishing their views unpaid, either verbatim or in edited form.

Readers who report regularly and reliably may be invited to join our Travellers' Panel. Members give us notice of their own travel plans; we suggest hotels that they might inspect, and contribute to the cost of accommodation.

The address to write to is:

Duncan Petersen Publishing Ltd
31 Ceylon Road
London W14 0YP
England.

Checklist

Please use a separate sheet of paper for each report; include your name and address on each report.

Your reports will be received with particular pleasure if they are typed, and if they are organized under the following headings:

Name of establishment
Town or village it is in, or nearest
Full address, including postcode
Date and duration of visit
The building and setting
The public rooms
The bedrooms and bathrooms
Comfort (chairs, beds, heat, light, hot water)
Standards of maintenance and housekeeping
Atmosphere, welcome and service
Food
Value for money

Manor house hotel, Brantôme (Dordogne)

Le Chatenet

This lovely 17thC manor house has prompted a steady flow of approving reports from readers over the years, and the latest gives the clearest possible view: 'We left wanting to stay longer, and we will certainly go back.' The appeal of the place stems not only from its rural surroundings – down a country track off the busy riverside road, blissfully far removed from the tourist bustle of Brantôme – but also from its informal atmosphere: despite evident investment in rich furnishings, the Laxtons clearly attach importance to the family-home feel. There are vases of fresh flowers on low tables, deep armchairs, and country antiques in both the sitting-room and breakfast room, which form part of the Laxtons' home. Bedrooms are spacious, with elegant decoration. In the cosy clubhouse there's an 'honesty' bar and room for wet-weather activities. Deckchairs are scattered invitingly in the garden beneath shady trees, and there is plenty of space for children.

Breakfast (with ten sorts of home-made *confiture*) is served on a terrace in fine weather, and guests may use an outdoor barbecue. If do-it-yourself doesn't appeal, there are some excellent restaurants nearby. The 'very cordial' welcome is 'enhanced by the dog'.
Nearby Brantôme; Bourdeilles (10 km) – château.

24310 Brantôme
Tel 05.53.05.81.08
Fax 05.53.05.85.52
Location 1.5 km SW of town, off D78; in large grounds with ample car parking
Meals breakfast
Prices FF
Rooms 8 double (6 twin), all with bath; 2 suites; on cottage with 2 double rooms; all rooms have central heating, phone; TV on request
Facilities sitting-room, breakfast room, clubhouse with billiards; heated swimming-pool, tennis
Credit cards MC, V
Children welcome if well behaved **Disabled** access easy; 2 ground-floor bedrooms, 1 specially equipped
Pets welcome if well behaved
Closed at times Nov to Apr
Proprietors Philippe and Magdeleine Laxton

Bordeaux and the Dordogne

Country hotel, Brantôme (Dordogne)

Domaine de la Roseraie

In the lush, green 'Venice of Périgord', this is a charming, mainly one-storey, renovated 17thC farmhouse with a tower, which our inspector found most welcoming and comfortable. The warm hospitality extends even to a free laundry service. It's the kind of hotel where departing guests give bouquets of flowers to Mme la Patronne – in this case Mme Roux. Due to hard work and constant upgrading, the hotel continues to get better and better. Future plans include having a swimming-pool and tennis courts ready for the summer of 1997. Rooms – all are on the ground floor and named after roses – are a delightful mix of bright fabrics and antiques; bathrooms are immaculate. A special half-timbered suite for families – called Prestige – has a gallery, a little wooden staircase and two double beds. There are two relaxing sitting-rooms, one for watching TV. The most recent addition to the hotel is a modestly-priced restaurant, serving traditional cuisine of the Périgord. M and Mme Roux, as well as being engaging and attentive hosts, have also taken it upon themselves to be vigilant guardians of the peace and quiet that has drawn painters, writers and nature lovers to the area over the ages.
Nearby Périgueux (20 km).

Route d'Angoulême
24310 Brantôme
Tel 05 53 05 84 74
Fax 05 53 05 77 94
Location in countryside; on a 4-hectare estate
Meals all
Prices FF
Rooms 6 double, 1 suite; 2 twin; all with bath, shower, phone, sat TV, heating, hairdryer
Facilities terrace, garden secure car parking
Credit cards AE, DC, MC, V
Children accepted
Disabled 1 room
Pets accepted
Closed 15th Jan to 15th March
Proprietors M and Mme Roux

Bordeaux and the Dordogne

Converted mill, Brantôme (Dordogne)

Moulin de l'Abbaye

Our visits to this exquisite little mill have always left us wishing to stay longer; why, we wonder, do we not hear from more readers about it? Could the Relais & Châteaux prices be to blame?

The setting is the thing. The shady riverside terrace, illuminated in the evening, is an idyllic place for a drink or a meal while admiring Brantôme's unusual angled bridge, the tower of the abbey or the swans gliding by. Wonderful views over the river and the old houses of one of the prettiest villages in France are also to be had from many of the bedrooms – all beautifully decorated and comfortably furnished (some have four-poster beds and antiques, others are more modern).

Traditional Périgord dishes with a *nouvelle* touch earn the restaurant 3 *toques* from Gault-Millau and a star from Michelin. The dining-room is as pleasant a place to enjoy this excellent cuisine as the terrace it leads to, though we can raise no enthusiasm for the 'Monet-style' colour scheme. There are fresh flowers, sparkling glass and silverware, and soft lighting in the evening. Staff are correct and courteous; service is efficient.

Nearby Monk's garden, belfry; Antonne-et-Trigonant (3 km) – 15thC Périgord manor; Bourdeilles (10 km) – château.

1 Route de Bourdeilles
24310 Brantôme
Tel 05.53.05.80.22
Location on edge of town, 20 km N of Périgueux; with garden, and ample car parking across road
Meals breakfast, lunch, dinner
Prices FFF
Rooms 17 double, 3 apartments, all with bath; all rooms have central heating, TV, minibar
Facilities dining-room, sitting-room
Credit cards AE, DC, MC, V
Children welcome
Disabled no special facilities
Pets dogs accepted
Closed Nov to May; restaurant only, Mon lunch
Manager M Dessum

Bordeaux and the Dordogne

Manor house hotel, Le Buisson-de-Cadouin (Dordogne)

Manoir de Bellerive

Our most recent report on this fine Napoléon III manor house embracingly sums up its attractions: 'Magnificent rooms, spectacular grounds, very friendly staff. Fabulous.' Set in a lovely, peaceful, formal park, with mature cedars, which stretches down to the banks of the Dordogne, the Bellerive epitomises the elegant *maison de campagne* one always hopes to find in the French countryside, but seldom does. Sunbeds and tables are liberally scattered over the lawns and a swimming-pool and tennis court are tucked away behind the trees. There is a balustraded first floor terrace, looking over the slow-moving river.

As you step inside the lofty entrance hall, you feel you have been transported back in time. The staircase sweeps up to spacious and very comfortable designer-decorated bedrooms, with period furnishings and delightful use of colour – most overlook the formal gardens or the river. Breakfast can be taken on the terrace. Meals here are memorable. Talented young chef, Eric Jung, has a way with fish and regional specialities. For six months of the year the hotel is also used as a conference centre. At other times, utter peace reigns. Owners M and Mme Clévenot are charming hosts.
Nearby Caves at Lascaux; Sarlat (30 km); *bastide* villages.

Route de Siorac
24480 Le Buisson-de-Cadouin
Tel 05 53 27 16 19
Fax 05 53 22 09 05
Location on the Dordogne river between Lalinde and Sarlat
Meals all
Prices FF-FFF
Rooms 16 double; 6 with twin beds; 8 with bath, 8 with shower; all with phone, heating, sat TV, minibar, trouser press, safe; 8 with air-conditioning
Facilities sitting-room; sauna; whirlpool bath; swimming-pool; tennis court; car parking
Credit cards AE, DC, MC, V
Children accepted
Disabled no special facilities
Pets accepted; 75F a day
Closed mid-Nov to mid-March
Proprietors M and Mme Clévenot

Bordeaux and the Dordogne

Village inn, Carennac (Lot)

Hostellerie Fénelon

This jolly-looking *logis* – all red roofs and window-boxes – in a lovely old village comes strongly recommended for Mme Raynal's warm welcome, the friendly and unobtrusive service of her staff, the 'very good home-style' cooking and excellent value for money. The place is a riot of flowers: at every window, beside the pool and around the terrace. Bedrooms are larger than usual for this price range and, though not particularly exciting, are clean and neat with reproduction furniture. From some rooms there is a beautiful view of the Dordogne river. Mme takes her bathrooms very seriously: they have been recently modernised and are spotless. French windows looking out over the river make the dining-room an especially pleasant place to linger over a meal. In the summer, guests dine outside on the terrace at the front of the hotel, which is shielded from the road by a tall hedge. Guy Raynal's *cuisine de terroir* is generous and satisfying – and commendably affordable. Even the continental breakfast is more copious than the norm. There is a small swimming-pool, surrounded by umbrella-shaded tables and chairs. All in all, first-class value in the budget range.
Nearby Carennac priory; Châteaux de Castelnau, Montal, Loubressac (10 km each); Rocamadour (30 km).

46110 Carennac
Tel 05 65 10 96 46
Fax 05 65 10 94 86
Location in centre of medieval village
Meals all
Prices F
Rooms 15 double; 1 twin; 10 with bath, 5 with shower; all with phone, TV, heating
Facilities terrace, pool, car parking
Credit cards AE, MC, V
Children accepted
Disabled access difficult
Pets accepted
Closed 8th Jan to 10th March
Proprietors M and Mme Raynal

Bordeaux and the Dordogne

Converted mill, Champagnac-de-Belair (Dordogne)

Le Moulin du Roc

A steady flow of approving reports from readers confirm the attractions of this delectable old walnut-oil mill, one of that rare breed of hotels that give you the sense of being pampered without costing £100 a night for a room. 'Absolutely stellar,' says the most recent – although the Moulin is less stellar than it used to be (these days it rates 'only' one Michelin star).

The setting on the banks of the Dronne is wonderfully romantic; the waterside gardens are lush, secluded, shady and bursting with colour. Inside the rough-stone 17thC building, old beams, fireplaces, mill machinery, fine old carved furniture, rich fabrics and massive oil-paintings – together with plenty of ornaments and flower arrangements – create a style that is highly individual, or even eccentric. Some may find it rather heavy. The same cannot be said of the food: in the land of *foie gras*, Alain Gardillou, who has taken over from his mother, manages to build on culinary traditions to produce remarkably light and inventive dishes. Breakfasts are a treat, with home-made rolls and jams, beautifully served. Bedrooms vary in size, but do not disappoint – pretty, cosy, with their full share of antiques.

Nearby Brantôme; Bourdeilles (15 km) – château.

24530 Champagnac-de-Belair
Tel 05.53.02.86.00
Fax 05.53.54.21.31
Location in hamlet, on D82 and D83, 6 km NE of Brantôme; with large garden and ample car parking
Meals breakfast, lunch, dinner
Prices FF
Rooms 10 double (2 twin), 4 suites; all with bath; all rooms have central heating, phone, TV, minibar
Facilities sitting-room, dining-room; heated swimming-pool, tennis court, terrace
Credit cards AE, DC, MC, V
Children welcome
Disabled 2 ground-floor rooms
Pets accepted
Closed 2 Jan to 8 Mar; restaurant only, Tue, Wed lunch
Proprietors M and Mme Gardillou

Bordeaux and the Dordogne

Manor house, Coly (Dordogne)

Manoir d'Hautegente

A reader describes this creeper-clad manor house as 'so good that I wouldn't tell you about it if it were not already in the guide'. We'll just have to hope that he doesn't mind our promotion of the Manoir – new to the guide a few years ago – to a full entry.

The house, set in beautiful wooded grounds, has been in the Hamelin family for about 300 years, and is now run by Edith Hamelin and her son Patrick. It was built as a forge in the 13thC, later became a mill (using the stream that runs beside it), was then embellished and turned into a family residence and was finally converted into a hotel – but with the feeling of a private house being skilfully retained. Public rooms and the spacious, comfortable bedrooms are imaginatively decorated with family antiques and paintings. Dinner in the pretty vaulted dining-room is a five-course affair – 'first-class cuisine' which inevitably includes home-produced *foie gras*, another of the Hamelins' commercial successes. Wines are reasonably priced.

In the pleasant grassy grounds there is a smart pool that gets plenty of sun. The Hamelins are natural hosts and a warm welcome awaits guests to their family home.

Nearby châteaux; Lascaux (15 km); Sarlat (25 km).

Coly
24120 Terrasson
Tel 05.53.51.68.03
Fax 05.53.50.38.52
Location in countryside, 6 km SE of Le Lardin on the D62; with grounds and car parking
Meals breakfast, dinner
Prices FF-FFF
Rooms 12 double, all with bath (2 twin); all rooms have central heating, phone; hairdryer, TV
Facilities dining-room, sitting-room; heated swimming-pool
Credit cards MC, V
Children welcome
Disabled 1 ground-floor room
Pets accepted if well behaved
Closed Nov to Easter
Proprietors Edith Hamelin and Patrick Hamelin

Bordeaux and the Dordogne

Farmhouse hotel, Florimont-Gaumiers (Dordogne)

La Daille

Another Dordogne establishment that combines the best of France and Britain. The mellow stone, red-roofed buildings are surrounded by gardens with glorious herbaceous borders that could only be the work of British green fingers. Rich local produce is transformed into wonderful light dishes that stand in sharp contrast to the typical Périgord menu.

British *emigrés* Barbara and Derek Vaughan Brown have been running this unusual establishment, in wonderful unspoiled and hilly countryside just south of the Dordogne, for nearly 20 years now – and have built up a regular local clientele for their afternoon teas and ambitious set dinners. La Daille is a small-scale *pension* catering for no more than 7 residents and 14 non-resident diners (half board obligatory, minimum stay three days unless you can sneak in a night or two between bookings).

The double bedrooms are in a modern single-storey building – thoroughly comfortable, with big bathrooms and terraces – across the garden from the original farmhouse, which contains the cool, rustic dining-room. The one (equally comfortable) single is in an old outbuilding.

Nearby golf, canoeing; Domme (15 km) – *bastide*; Sarlat (25 km).

Florimont-Gaumiers
24250 Domme
Tel 05.53.28.40.71
Location in countryside, 2 km S of Gaumiers (signposted from village); in large grounds with ample car parking
Meals breakfast, afternoon tea, dinner
Prices F
Rooms 3 double (2 twin), one single, all with bath or shower; all rooms have central heating
Facilities dining-room, terrace
Credit cards not accepted
Children accepted over 7
Disabled access difficult
Pets not accepted
Closed Oct to 1 May
Proprietors Mr and Mrs Derek Vaughan Brown

Bordeaux and the Dordogne

Château hotel, Gramat (Lot)

Château de Roumégouse

We're grateful that this exceptional Relais and Châteaux has kept its prices *relatively* reasonable, for this 19thC château, much loved by Charles de Gaulle and on the top of a hill, is charming. Moreover, the Lainés are the perfect hosts, creating an ambience that is relaxed and romantic (fresh flowers in every room) and never stuffy. Bedrooms bear the arms of local families and are individually furnished, each one prettier than the next. Styles range from 'Rignac', warmly done in ochre and indigo with hand-painted armoire, to the large 'Roumégouse', with an imposing Rococo bedstead. 'Auvergne' is in the castle's tower. The public rooms are elegant and filled with light – and flowers. The dining-room has a handsome stone fireplace. When the weather is warm, meals are served on the balustraded terrace, which has panoramic views of the Lot valley. On summer nights, in soft lamplight, this makes an entrancing place to dine, with white parasols and white linen. In the land of the truffle, be prepared for the rich fare of the area. In the *fin-de-siècle* wooded park is a swimming-pool with wide paved surrounds and a round stone folly which is the château's own Tower of Babel.

Nearby Rocamadour (18 km); Carennac (30 km).

Rignac
46500 Gramat
Tel 05 65 33 63 81
Fax 05 65 33 71 18
Location in a 5-hectare wooded park with car parking
Meals all
Prices FF-FFF
Rooms 14 double and 1 suite; all with bath, shower, phone, TV, heating, minibar
Facilities terrace; swimming-pool; helipad
Credit cards AE, DC, MC, V
Children accepted
Disabled no special facilities
Pets accepted
Closed 1st Nov to Easter
Directors M and Mme Lainé

Bordeaux and the Dordogne

Château hotel, Lacave (Lot)

Château de la Treyne

We've had our eye on this little château beside the Dorgogne since an inspector came back a few years ago with a report littered with emphatically underscored adjectives – 'gorgeous ... impeccable ... exceptionally comfortable'. Of course, it is not cheap; perhaps we should be grateful that elevation to Relais & Châteaux status has not pushed prices up further.

Michèle Gombert-Devals' house has made a splendid small hotel. It starts with the advantage of a beautiful position, in woods on a low cliff cut by the meandering river Dordogne. But the compelling attraction of the château is the near-ideal balance struck between the impressiveness of a fortified manor-house and the intimacy of a genuine home. The building dates from the early 14th C, but was substantially rebuilt in the 1600s; it is now tastefully equipped with a happy mix of furnishings – comfy sofas in front of an open fire, as well as grand antiques.

There are long walks to enjoy in the grounds, and a very beautiful formal garden before which you can take breakfast. Excellent regional food is served – on the delightful terrace perched above the river in good weather.

Nearby Souillac – abbey church; Rocamadour, Sarlat.

Lacave
46200 Souillac
Tel 05.65.27.60.60
Fax 05.65.27.60.70
Location 3 km W of village on D43, 6 km SE of Souillac; in large grounds beside river, with ample car parking
Meals all
Prices FFF-FFFF
Rooms 14 double, all with bath, central heating, air-conditioning, phone, TV
Facilities 3 sitting-rooms, dining-room, bar, billiard room, meeting-room; sauna, swimming-pool, tennis
Credit cards AE, DC, MC, V
Children welcome
Disabled access difficult
Pets accepted if well behaved
Closed 15 Nov to Easter
Proprietor Mme Michèle Gombert-Devals

Bordeaux and the Dordogne

Riverside hotel, Lacave (Lot)

Hôtel du Pont de l'Ouysse

The *raison d'être* of this peaceful, small *auberge* is its magnificent dining terrace overlooking the river, shaded by horse chestnut and lime trees. The approach, via a long, private drive, gives a first impression of total seclusion. (This privacy is especially valued by guests; our inspector spotted a celebrated French news anchorman on a recent visit.) There's a riverside walk with benches and a new pool discreetly tucked away from the main bustle of the hotel. There is not a sound here of traffic, only bird-song and the murmuring of the river.

The large house has been in Mme Chambon's family for generations and still feels in many ways like a private home. Rooms are decorated with pretty English wallpapers and matching fabrics; some have angled ceilings and authentic beams. It is always a good sign when the restaurant draws local as well as hotel guests and Daniel Chambon's cooking packs the dining-room with people from as far away as Sarlat. His creative talents are complemented by his liberal use of fresh local produce (which includes eel from the Ouysse). Our reporter was enchanted: 'Beautiful setting, great food and charming hosts.'

Nearby Souillac (8 km); Sarlat (35 km); Rocamadour (30 km).

46200 Lacave
Tel 05 65 37 87 04
Fax 05 65 32 77 41
Location in 5-hectare grounds on the river Ouysse
Meals all
Prices FF
Rooms 12 double, 2 suites; all with bath, phone, TV, heating, minibar, hairdryer, safe
Facilities terrace, pool
Credit cards AE, DC, MC, V
Children accepted
Disabled no special facilities
Pets accepted
Closed Jan and Feb; 15th Nov to 15th Dec
Proprietors M and Mme Chambon

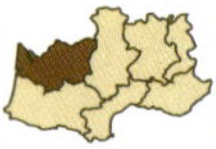

Bordeaux and the Dordogne

Farmhouse hotel, Mauroux (Lot)

Hostellerie Le Vert

Le Vert goes from strength to strength. The attractions of this secluded 17thC farmhouse have been greatly increased by the construction of a swimming-pool. Whatever the changes, however, it will doubtless remain the kind of hotel you look forward to returning to at the end of the day; it also looks set to become the kind you're disinclined to leave at all.

There is just a small side-door to lead you inside. Within, all is original stone walls and beams. The dining-room opens out on to a terrace with wide views; through an arch at one end is a small sitting-room – ideal for an aperitif. The bedrooms are all comfortably and tastefully modernized, and have lovely views. The largest are quite grand and furnished with antiques. But the most attractive are in the little annexe a couple of yards from the entrance – the lower one stone-vaulted, the upper one beamed, with a marble floor. The garden has chairs and tables, and is improving in colour despite dry summers. The owners are a friendly and hard-working couple – M Philippe cooks (interestingly and competently), Mme Philippe serves (and speaks excellent English).

Nearby Bonaguil (15 km) – château; Biron castle (35 km); Monpazier (50 km) – *bastide*; Cahors (50 km) – medieval bridge.

Mauroux
46700 Puy-l'Evêque
Tel 05.65.36.51.36
Location in countryside, off D5 10 km SW of Puy-l'Evêque; 10 km SE of Fumel; in garden, with ample private car parking
Meals breakfast, lunch, dinner
Prices F
Rooms 7 double, all with bath or shower; all have central heating, phone, TV
Facilities dining-room, sitting-room, terrace, swimming-pool
Credit cards AE, MC, V
Children welcome – children's menu 50F
Disabled no special facilities
Pets welcome at extra charge
Closed mid Nov to mid Feb
Proprietors Eva and Bernard Philippe

Bordeaux and the Dordogne

Château hotel, Pauillac (Gironde)

Château Cordeillan-Bages

The restaurant and terrace at Cordeillan-Bages look directly out on to rows of vines – neighbours are Latour, Lafite, Mouton-Rothschild and many other distinguished names in the history of wine. Built in the purest 17thC style, the château is in the heart of the Médoc. (There's a small boutique selling good vintages). The lovely, pale-stone, well-proportioned single-storey house was completely restored in 1989 and the decoration is stylish and restful. There is something of the feel of an English country house about the intimate sitting-rooms and elegant dining-room. The bedrooms are very comfortable, with the sure hand of the interior designer given full rein. In the kitchen, chef Thierry Marx uses his skills to create new dishes based on seasonal produce, as well as traditional regional food. The wine list is encyclopaedic. The château is home to the *Ecole de Bordeaux*, which offers a wide choice of courses for both professional and amateur wine lovers and organizes visits to other vineyards in the area. A Relais and Châteaux, the hotel slightly lacks the character it might have in private hands, but it is a charming house and the high standard of service lives up to 4-star expectations.
Nearby Château Mouton-Rothschild (5 km) Bordeaux (40 km).

Route des Châteaux
33250 Pauillac
Tel 05 56 59 24 24
Fax 05 56 59 01 89
Location in wine village on D2, 40 km N of Bordeaux; on 3 hectares of vineyards
Meals all
Prices FFFF
Rooms 24 double, 1 suite; 9 twin; all with bath, phone, sat TV, heating, minibar, hairdryer, safe
Facilities sitting-rooms, terrace, parking
Credit cards AE, DC, V
Children accepted
Disabled all facilities
Pets small ones accepted
Closed 8th Dec to 1st Feb
Manager M Cazes

Bordeaux and the Dordogne

Converted mill, Poudenas (Lot-et-Garonne)

Le Moulin de la Belle Gasconne

This was a *coup de foudre* for our experienced inspector: 'After half a century of travelling across the world I have a dream of what a French *auberge* should be. This is it – and Mme Garcia's passion for the place shows through in all of it.' Firstly, the building: a beautifully-restored 14thC stone mill on a stream (the Gélise) by a bridge nestling below an ancient hill town. Secondly: serenely peaceful green countryside with trees and a charmingly wild garden with a swimming-pool. Thirdly: an imaginatively created cool dining-room, exquisite (not too big) bedrooms and highly individual bathrooms or showers. Fourthly: superb food. Mme Marie-Claude Garcia incarnates five generations of cooks and is passionate about her kitchen; she is the author of *La Cuisine de Passion - Gardienne des Traditions du Sud Ouest.* Sadly, she lost her husband in the early part of 1996, but, fortunately for us, she has kept her sense of mission. Fifthly: excellent wines and armagnac. This, enthuses our inspector, is a gem, where living is an art. Connoisseurs and those with cravings for *foie gras* will feel most comfortable here. There is a also a romantic terrace on which to appreciate Mme Garcia's *Grand Repas Gascon* (285F), or her less expensive menu.
Nearby château of Poudenas; *bastide* villages; Condom (19 km).

Meals 47170 Poudenas
Tel 05 53 65 71 58
Fax 05 53 65 87 39
Location on the river's edge in a village 17 km from Nérac
Meals Breakfast, lunch, dinner
Prices FF
Rooms 6 double; 5 with bath, 1 with shower; all with phone, TV; hairdryer on request
Facilities swimming-pool; table tennis in garden; fishing
Credit cards AE, DC, MC, V
Children accepted
Disabled no special facilities
Pets accepted
Closed 7th Jan to 10th Feb
Proprietor Mme Garcia

Bordeaux and the Dordogne

Village hotel, Puymirol (Lot-et-Garonne)

Les Loges de l'Aubergade

'Excellence par excellence' enthused a visitor to this handsome former residence of the Counts of Toulouse, dating from the 13thC and in a little fortified village. The lodestones to Puymirol are chef Michel Trama (two Michelin stars) for his superb food, wine and cigars, and his wife, Maryse, with whom he has created this international-class hotel-restaurant. The building has stone walls, high ceilings, beams, a 17thC oak staircase and is decorated with impeccable style. The extensive kitchens are impressive and full of activity with M Trama very much in personal charge. A unique feature is a large smoking-room with a glass fronted fully-humidified cabinet containing a collection of very best Cuban cigars – not for show but for smoking.

A terrace garden, leading off the dining-room, has attractive canvas sunshades and is discreetly illuminated through trees and bushes after dark. Bedrooms are large and elegant and bathrooms have whirlpool baths. The feeling of the whole building is of intense light and airiness, predominantly white (much original stone), with white furniture, offset with green and the colour of floral decoration

Nearby Agen (17 km); Moissac (32 km); Villeneuve-sur-Lot (31 km).

52 rue Royale,
47270 Puymirol
Tel 05 53 95 31 46
Fax 05 53 95 33 80
Location in the middle of a small, fortified village; 20 km E of Agen
Meals all
Prices FFF-FFFF
Rooms 11 double; bath, shower, phone, sat TV, air-conditioning, minibar, video, hairdryer; all with whirlpool bath or massage shower
Facilities terrace, parking; garage
Credit cards AE, DC, MC, V
Children accepted
Disabled 2 rooms on ground floor
Pets accepted
Closed 5 weeks in Feb/Mar
Proprietors M and Mme Trama

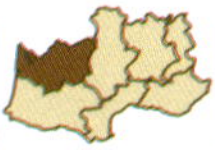

Bordeaux and the Dordogne

Converted stables, Rocamadour (Lot)

Domaine de la Rhue

We are particularly impressed with this delightful small hotel, an imaginative conversion of 19thC stables (the entry salon, in which breakfast is served, still has its original paving stones, heavy timbers and a roaring, open fire on chilly evenings). Peacefully set amid rolling countryside, out of sight of any other building apart from the château next door, it is hard to believe it is only a few kilometres away from the tourist trap of Rocamadour. Rooms are decorated with style and inspiration, but totally in keeping with the building's original use, and are named after equine colourings. They have large, modern bathrooms. Several are suitable for families and some have kitchenettes. One of the prettiest – in a red-shuttered cottage with a beamed ceiling – is extremely good value.

The English-speaking owners, Eric and Christine Jooris, are charming and welcoming hosts. They are happy to provide cold snack lunches, which can be eaten beside the swimming- pool. M Jooris is a passionate hot-air balloon pilot and can arrange for guests to see Rocamadour from the air. The lack of a restaurant will suit free spirits; there are plenty of places to dine locally.
Nearby Rocamadour (7 km); Carennac (20 km); Loubressac (20 km).

46200 Rocamadour
Tel 05 65 33 71 50
Fax 05 65 33 72 48
Location in countryside, on the N140 7 km N of Rocamadour
Meals breakfast, light lunch
Prices FF
Rooms 11 double, I family room; 10 with bath, 2 with shower; all with phone, heating, fan; 6 with hairdryer; 4 with minibar; 2 with kitchen- ette; TV on request
Facilities sitting-room; swimming-pool; car parking
Credit cards MC, V
Children accepted
Disabled no special facilities
Pets accepted; 30F a day
Closed mid-Oct to Easter
Proprietors M and Mme Jooris

Bordeaux and the Dordogne

Village hotel, St-Cirq-Lapopie (Lot)

La Pélissaria

Recent reports leave us in no doubt that the Matuchets' distinctive little hotel is as compelling as ever. And the chances of finding a room vacant have increased since they bought an old house next door to the main one, providing three additional large bedrooms (two double beds in each).

The 13thC house clings to the steep hillside on the edge of the lovely medieval hilltop village of St-Cirq-Lapopie. It was lovingly restored by the Matuchets themselves, and its quirky character is such that you descend the stairs to the bedrooms, which look out on to the tiny garden and enjoy stunning views over the Lot valley. The bedrooms – two of them detached from the house, down the garden – are light, airy and comfortable, with close attention to detail in the furnishings.

Dinner, served in the elegant and intimate beamed dining-room (with roaring log fire on cold nights) is adventurous and delicious; Madame does all the cooking, so the choice of dishes is naturally limited. M Matuchet is a musician, and tapes of his music provide a background to dinner. Breakfast is served *alfresco* or in your room if you prefer.

Nearby Pech-Merle caves and museum; Cahors (35 km).

St-Cirq-Lapopie
46330 Cabrerets
Tel 05.65.31.25.14
Fax 05.65.30.25.52
Location in village, 30 km E of Cahors; with garden; car parking difficult
Meals breakfast, dinner
Prices FF
Rooms 8 double, 6 with bath, 2 with shower (4 twin); 2 suites with bath; all rooms have phone, TV
Facilities dining-room, sitting-room; small swimming-pool
Credit cards MC, V
Children welcome
Disabled 1 adapted bedroom
Pets accepted
Closed mid-Nov to Apr; restaurant only, Thu and Fri
Proprietor Marie-Françoise Matuchet

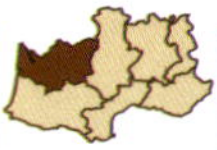

Bordeaux and the Dordogne

Village inn, St-Saud-Lacoussière (Dordogne)

Hostellerie Saint Jacques

The more we learn about the Babayous' enterprise, the more thoroughly impressed we are by their sure understanding of holidaymakers' needs and priorities.

The front of the creeper-clad 18thC building gives little clue to what lies within – or, more to the point, what lies behind: the Babayous' 'summer sitting-room', which consists of lovely sloping gardens, with masses of colourful flowers, a fair-sized pool, tennis court and plenty of shade and space for children. Inside there is an unusually large dining-room/bar decorated in fresh summery colours, with big windows which open on to the terrace above the garden. All the bedrooms are comfortable, spacious and attractively decorated; several can accommodate families.

The food is rich and varied; even the basic menu is probably enough to satisfy most appetites. A buffet breakfast/brunch is served in the garden or by the pool. Occasionally there are lively evenings with dancing and games, or communal dinners devoted to exploration of regional cuisine. Not your cup of tea? Just give it a try: you might be surprised.

Nearby Montbrun (15 km) – fortress; Brantôme (30 km) – monks' garden, Château de Richemont; Rochechouart (45 km).

24470 St-Saud-Lacoussière
Tel 05.53.56.97.21
Fax 05.53.56.91.33
Location in quiet village, 30 km N of Brantôme; with garden and car parking
Meals breakfast/brunch, lunch, dinner
Prices F-FF
Rooms 22 double (7 twin), 2 suites, all with bath or shower, central heating, phone; 10 have TV and minibar
Facilities 2 dining-rooms, bar, TV room; swimming-pool, tennis
Credit cards MC, V
Children very welcome
Disabled no special facilities
Pets accepted
Closed mid-Oct to Mar; restaurant closed to non-residents Sun dinner and Mon
Proprietor Jean-Pierre Babayou

Bordeaux and the Dordogne

Converted mill, Touzac (Lot)

Hostellerie de la Source Bleue

Set peacefully beside the Lot in a grove of weeping willows, this hotel is an oasis of verdant tranquillity in a quiet corner of Quercy. The property has been in the family of M Bouyou for more than 600 years and consists of three mills built in the 11thC, 13thC and 17thC. The trio of large rooms under the eaves in the main 700-year-old paper-mill have been renovated with particular sensitivity and taste, and even the lowest-priced rooms are reasonably spacious and endowed with charm. A smaller mill is used for art exhibitions. The hotel's rustic dining-room and pool are added attractions. A terrace overlooks a cobalt-coloured pool – 'the blue spring' – bubbling from an underground spring rich in magnesium.

Guests have the freedom of a large park; there are long walks along paths following the river and through a plantation of giant bamboo and a birch forest. Smaller guests will enjoy the children's garden and the hotel has a leisure centre, a library, a room for tea, and a boat. There is also a kitchen garden, and home-grown cherries, apricots, hazelnuts and raspberries feature at mealtimes. Salmon and *rôti de lotte* in a fresh tomato sauce are specialities of the house.

Nearby Puy L'Evêque (20 km); Cahors (48 km).

Moulin de Leygues
46700 Touzac
Tel 05 65 36 52 01
Fax 05 65 24 65 69
Location in 3-hectare grounds on the banks of the Lot
Meals all
Prices F
Rooms 17 double; 6 with twin beds; 16 with bath, 1 with shower; all with phone, TV, heating
Facilities swimming-pool; sitting rooms; terrace; fitness centre; sauna; boat; parking
Credit cards AE, DC, MC, V
Children accepted
Disabled 1 room
Pets accepted; 30F a day
Closed Jan to April
Proprietors M and Mme Bouyou

Bordeaux and the Dordogne

Village hotel, Trémolat (Dordogne)

Le Vieux Logis

We continue to list this glorious old hotel, for our money one of the most civilized in a region with many attractive hotels, despite the fact that (to judge by our postbag) precious few readers are inclined to pay its prices. (If you decide to treat yourself to a stay here, do let us have a report.)

The Giraudel-Destords have lived in this complex of farm and village houses for nearly 400 years. The part which is now the dining-room once held pigs and wine barrels. Now, all has been designer-decorated to produce comfort of a high degree. The bedrooms are particularly delightful: individually furnished and very cosy in a sophisticated rustic style, with fine materials and furniture; some have four-poster beds. Public rooms are elegant and comfortable, and there are plenty of quiet nooks; the small salon has an open fire, and there are fine antiques throughout. The galleried dining-room is very attractive, and looks out on to the green and flowery garden, where you can have breakfast. The classic and modern cooking of Pierre-Jean Duribreux is excellent (two *toques* from Gault-Millau).

Nearby Les Eyzies-de-Tayac (25 km) – National Prehistoric Museum; Monpazier (30 km) – *bastide*; Beynac (30 km).

24510 Trémolat
Tel 05.53.22.80.06
Fax 05.53.22.84.89
Location in village 15 km SW of Le Bugue; with garden and private car parking
Meals breakfast, lunch, dinner
Prices FFF-FFFF+
Rooms 24 double (13 twin), all with bath; all rooms have central heating, phone, TV, minibar
Facilities 2 dining-rooms, 3 sitting-rooms, bar, conference room, pool
Credit cards AE, DC, MC, V
Children welcome
Disabled 1 adapted room; easy access to dining-room
Pets welcome
Closed never
Proprietor M Bernard Giraudel-Destord

Bordeaux and the Dordogne

Château hotel, Vieux Mareuil (Dordogne)

Château de Vieux Mareuil

Behind the thick, ivy-clad stone walls of this 15thC fortified house lies a stylish little hotel, prettily decorated with plenty of attention to detail. Our inspector predicts that with an intelligent new owner, friendly and dedicated staff and reduced prices, this delightful hotel in the Périgord will collect plenty of new admirers. The château's estate is as attractive as the house; there are 20 hectares of parkland with winding paths through woods and meadows and cliffs and caves.

Most of the bedrooms are in the hotel's renovated wing, many with wicker furniture and decorated in fresh, bright colours. But for sheer atmosphere it is difficult to beat the two large rooms in the tower, which have exposed stone, authentic beams and interesting little nooks and crannies. The scale everywhere is small and intimate. The food is well above average and the gifted young chef is a master of regional specialities. (His *tatin de foie gras* is superb). Service is discreet but friendly and the staff most anxious to please. There is a heated swimming-pool alongside the house, with a gravelled terrace.

Nearby Brantôme (13 km); Châteaux de la Baronnie de Mareuil, de Richemont, de Bourdeilles, de Puyguilhem; Périgueux (40 km).

Route Angoulême-Périgueux
24340 Vieux Mareuil
Tel 05 53 60 77 15
Fax 05 53 56 49 33
Location on large country estate with woods and meadows
Meals all
Prices FF
Rooms 14 double; 6 with twin beds; all with bath, phone, heating, sat TV, minibar, hairdryer
Facilities private park, heated pool, sitting-rooms, car parking
Credit cards AE, MC, V
Children accepted
Disabled 1 room
Pets accepted
Closed 15th Oct to 15th March
Proprietor M Desprez

Country house, Villeréal (Lot-et-Garonne)

Château de Ricard

Everything is immaculate about this renovated *castella de petit seigneur* built in H-form with four *pigeonnier*-style turrets in 1830 (it opened to guests in mid-1995) and elegantly set in spacious grounds. The garden has manicured lawns, abundant floral display under mature trees, weeping willows reflected in lakes and even a swamp cypress.

In the main house, there is a fine salon, library, billiard room (French), dining-room and laundry facilities – all for use by guests as in their own home. Upstairs are three magnificent bedrooms – with excellent bathrooms. The stable block has been cleverly adapted for a charming breakfast room overlooking one of the lakes, a dining-room and two suites. The owners are connoisseurs of fabrics, wall coverings and tiles and their taste and expertise embellish all the rooms down to the last detail. Bed linen is changed daily; books are everywhere and for use. Breakfast is sumptuous, whether taken inside or on the large terrace by the pool and is included in the room price. Evening meals are by arrangement for the very reasonable, inclusive price of 150F for good regional food and wine. Some may find it a bit too tidy.

Nearby Bastide de Villeréal (1 km); Bergerac (30 km).

Route de Beaumont
47210 Villeréal
Tel 05 53 36 61 02
Fax 05 53 36 61 65
Location in countryside on D676 N of Villeréal with car parking
Meals breakfast; dinner 4 nights a week
Prices FF
Rooms 3 double and 2 suites; all with bath; suites with terrace
Facilities swimming-pool; tennis; billiards; fishing
Credit cards not yet
Children accepted
Disabled access difficult
Pets not accepted
Closed 1st Nov to Easter
Proprietors M and Mme Deguilhem

The South-West

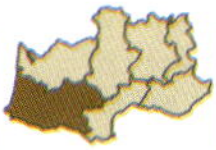

Village hotel, Aïnhoa (Pyrénées-Atlantiques)

Hôtel Ohantzea

This is by some margin the cheapest of our main recommendations in the Pyrénées-Atlantiques, and accordingly simple – but no less charming for that. The timbered and shuttered building is set on the road that runs through the attractive mountain village of Cambo-les-Bains, renowned for its mild climate – Edmond Rostand, author of *Cyrano de Bergerac*, came here to take the spa waters and liked it so much that he built a house nearby – see below.

It has been in the Ithurria family for three centuries and dates from the 17thC. It was originally a farm, but it is now very much a family house with old furniture dotted about, satisfyingly rustic and tasteful throughout – uneven wooden floors, beamed ceilings and family possessions. Bedrooms are notably spacious, some with balconies. The menus offer fair value and the dining-room is pleasant enough. "This is not a modern house" says Mme Ithurria in a pleasantly self-effacing way, "and we have no 'formula' – except to provide the atmosphere of a family home and fair prices."

Nearby Villa Arnaga, Rostand's house, on the D932 a short distance north of town; St-Pée-sur-Nivelle (10 km); Sare (10 km) – cog railway.

Aïnhoa
64250 Cambo-les-Bains
Tel 05.59.29.90.50
Location in middle of village, 10 km SW of Cambo-les-Bains; with garden and car parking behind
Meals breakfast, lunch, dinner
Prices rooms F; menus 120F-220F
Rooms 10 double, 9 with bath and shower (3 twin); all rooms have central heating, phone
Facilities sitting-room, dining-room
Credit cards AE, DC, MC, V
Children welcome
Disabled no special facilities
Pets accepted
Closed Dec and Jan
Proprietor M Ithurria

The South-West

Village hotel, Barcus (Pyrénées-Atlantiques)

Hôtel Chilo

It is well worth making a detour to enjoy the delights of this small hotel on the borders of the verdant Basque and Béarn country. The expertise of three generations has created a place of welcome, comfort and wonderful food. Rooms are attractively furnished and are colourful and light with well-equipped, brightly-tiled bathrooms (some with whirlpool baths). There is a room for the physically-handicapped on the ground floor; other bedrooms on the first and second floors have superb views over rolling wooded countryside. The garden is spacious and elegant, with an attractive swimming pool, with paved and lawned surround. Public rooms inside include a sizeable salon with large TV system, also a bar with open fireplace. The food is exceptional: visitors come especially from the Atlantic coast and from Paris for meals prepared with imagination and refinement under the guidance of M Chilo. Fresh game, fruit and vegetables are collected every day from the market, in what has become a family ritual over the generations. This is a refreshing, reasonably-priced, efficient and very enjoyable stopping-place for the traveller and the Chilo family specialize in a warm Basque welcome.

Nearby Pau; the Spanish border.

64130 Barcus
Tel 05 59 28 90 79
Fax 05 59 28 93 10
Location on D24 between Oloron Ste Marie and Mauléon
Meals all
Prices F-FF
Rooms 7 double and 3 family rooms; 6 with bath, 4 with shower; all with phone, heating; some with TV and hairdryer

Facilities swimming-pool, garden, terrace, secure car parking
Children accepted
Disabled 1 room
Pets dogs accepted
Closed 15th Jan -10th Feb
Proprietor M Pierre Chilo

The South-West

Château guest-house, Camon (Ariège)

Château de Camon

Classed as a historic monument, the Château de Camon has evolved, through a history of sackings, a flood and other dramatic events, alongside a Benedictine abbey, from which the monks finally fled during the Revolution. It came into the family of the present owner, M du Pont, an interior designer, in 1848. In a lovely old village of red-tiled roofs on the road to Spain, much of it is 16thC, with a huge, stone spiral staircase, high corridors with decorated beams, magnificent walls and old floor-tiles. The *salons* for house guests are grand – decorated and furnished in 18thC style. Our reporter slept in a curtained, four-poster bed; the big, modern bathroom, teak panelling and cupboards, has large windows overlooking terraced gardens down to elegant tree-scattered lawns, where there is a discreet swimming-pool.

A delightful inner court – where guests may sit after dinner – with lawn, shrubs and flowers, is enclosed by the walls of a church, the cloisters of the abbey and the windowed, arcaded corridor of the château. (M du Pont plans to turn it into a white garden.) Guests eat together at a long table with their host.

Nearby Mirepoix (12 km); Foix (45 km); Toulouse, Andorra (110 km).

09500 Mirepoix
Tel 05 61 68 28 28
Fax 05 61 68 81 56
Location in country village 12 km SW of Mirepoix
Meals breakfast; dinner
Prices FF-FFF (breakfast included); dinner on reservation 300F
Rooms 8 double, 1 suite; 6 with bath, 3 with shower
Facilities swimming-pool; park; fishing in grounds; car parking
Credit cards AE, EC, MC, V
Children accepted
Disabled no facilities
Pets not accepted
Closed 1st Nov to Easter
Proprietor M du Pont

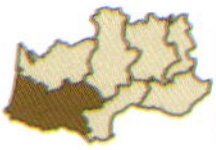

The South-West

Seaside guest-house, Ciboure (Pyrénées-Atlantiques)

Lehen Tokia

Lehen Tokia means 'first house' in Basque – it is a highly unusual and individual private house, built in 1925, with many art deco features (including stained glass by Jacques Grüber). Set on a hill, with views over the harbour of Ciboure and St-Jean-de-Luz, it is a classified historic monument and a splendid example of neo-Basque architecture.

The present owner, M Taboulet-Gould, was born in the house and returned to settle in Ciboure from New York in 1990; his wife is a painter from the Dordogne. The couple's personal belongings are everywhere on display: paintings, silver, books, glass, small bronzes and knick-knacks. It is very refined – and yet cosy – and for this reason children are not normally very welcome. What it lacks in spaciousness it makes up for in style. The small dining-room has an elegant Basque dresser with china plates and a fireplace and all the rooms are pleasingly comfortable. There's a small rose garden, a swimming-pool, a pretty summerhouse, and a terrace with delightful views. Lunch and dinner can be provided by prior arrangement – home cooking at around 100F for lunch and 120F for dinner. Sometimes paella is on menu.

Nearby St-Jean-de-Luz; Spanish border; Biarritz (16 km).

Chemin Achotarreta
64500 St-Jean-de-Luz
Tel 05 59 47 18 16
Fax 05 59 47 38 04
Location in a residential street, within walking distance of the beach and town centre
Meals breakfast; lunch and dinner on request
Prices FF-FFF
Rooms 5 double, 1 suite; all with phone, TV; 4 with bath, 4 with shower
Facilities sitting-rooms, garden, terrace, swimming-pool; street parking
Credit cards EC, MC, V
Children not accepted
Disabled no facilities
Pets no
Closed never
Proprietors M and Mme Taboulet-Gould

The South-West

Town hotel, Condom (Gers)

Hôtel des Trois Lys

Jeannette Manet will welcome you warmly to her lovingly-restored 18thC house, with cream local limestone walls and white shutters, and restrained elegant decoration within. Our inspector found this a remarkable oasis of calm and quiet in the middle of a busy market town – the capital of Armagnac country.

One entrance to the hotel is in a semi-pedestrian street and the other through a hillside courtyard, which provides secure private car parking and a discreetly walled-off swimming-pool area. The interior is light and restful, pleasantly furnished and with many original features – Versailles parquet floors, moulded wood panelling and a fine, old, wide, stone staircase with wrought iron railing. Bedrooms are spacious and smart, with antique or reproduction furniture and fresh flowers. Some are panelled, with original alcoves. Mme Manet is a caring host, dedicated to her *métier* and paying great attention to detail. A new feature is the restaurant, which occupies two rooms (one was formerly the *salon*) and the menu has local specialities fresh from the market (such as *foie gras* and *magret de canard).* Fish is delivered twice daily. A charming small hotel of great character.

Nearby Cathédrale St-Pierre; Musée de l'Armagnac.

38 rue Gambetta
32100 Condom
Tel 05 62 28 33 33
Fax 05 62 28 41 85
Location in town centre
Meals all
Prices FF
Rooms 10; 8 with bath; all with heating, phone, TV, hairdryer
Facilities pool; terrace; secure car parking
Credit cards AE, EC, MC, V
Children accepted
Disabled 1 room
Pets accepted
Closed Feb
Proprietor Mme Manet

Medieval inn, Cordes-sur-Ciel (Tarn)

Le Grand Écuyer

At the instigation of the novelist Prosper Mérimée, this former hunting lodge of the Counts of Toulouse was classified as a historic monument in the 19thC. It has been transformed into a comfortable and dependable hotel, with stone walls, beamed ceilings, heavy oak antique furniture, oil paintings, tapestry upholstery, suits of armour, paved floors, rich damask and velvet wall coverings, blackamoor lampholders and four-poster beds. Parts of it are rather gloomy, though the bedrooms are quiet and inviting (if you like monumental stone fireplaces), with modern bathrooms.

Cordes-sur-Ciel – a remarkably preserved 13thC fortified hilltop village, with little cobbled streets and a busy tourist attraction – is the gastronomic domain of pastry chef Yves Thuriès, who has a Michelin star and is something of a celebrity. Le Grand Écuyer is his base, though recent visitors feel he might be doing less in the kitchen now than in the past. The service is excellent and the chandeliered, plum-coloured dining-room has been conceived as the prestigious setting for his cuisine. Our reporter dined well, and was particularly struck by the helpfulness and knowledge of the wine waiter.

Nearby Fôret Grésigne (15 km); Albi (25 km); Toulouse (80 km).

Rue Voltaire
81170 Cordes-sur-Ciel
Tel 05 63 56 01 03
Fax 05 63 56 18 83
Location in middle of village 25 km NW of Albi; with public car parking nearby
Meals all
Prices FF-FFF
Rooms 12 double, 1 suite; all with bath; all rooms have phone, TV, heating, minibar, hairdryer; some have air-conditioning
Facilities 2 dining-rooms; breakfast room; sitting-room; bar
Credit cards AE, DC, MC, V
Children accepted
Disabled no special facilities
Pets accepted
Closed Nov to Easter
Proprietor Yves Thuriès

The South-West

Country hotel, Cuq-Toulza (Tarn)

Cuq-en-Terrasses

When we looked at this once semi-abandoned old presbytery some time ago we thought it was a full entry in the making: under conversion since 1990 by a couple of London designers, it seemed to have great potential. Now Cuq-en-Terrasses has, indeed, made it. We take our hats off to Tim and Zara Whitmore for their charming and successful restoration. The house, in a hilltop village square, is on a series of south-facing levels – from the street downwards – with further terraces of garden below.

The entrance hall leads to the upstairs rooms via a balustraded staircase and a superb beamed ceiling (uncovered during the building work). Kitchen, dining-room and beautiful outside terrace (with barbecue) for summer meals are two floors down. The swimming-pool is on another terrace. All quite stunning. The decoration and furnishing are original without eccentricity – clean, fresh, colourful. Tim Whitmore has worked for Biba and Paul McCartney, and his wife, Zara Nutting, is an artist – and dedicated cook. The *table d'hôte* dinner for guests is chosen with care and prepared with skill. The view is lovely, the welcome warm but unobtrusive; an ideal place in which to relax and enjoy the quiet.
Nearby Castres (35 km); Toulouse (37 km).

Cuq Le Château
81470 Cuq-Toulza
Tel 05 63 82 54 00
Fax 05 63 82 54 11
Location in a hilltop hamlet by the church; 3 km from Cuq-Toulza
Meals all (by reservation)
Prices FF-FFF
Rooms 7 double, 1 family; 6 with bath, 2 with shower; all with phone, TV; hairdryer on request
Facilities pool; laundry service; badminton; parking; tennis 1 km
Credit cards DC, MC, V
Children accepted
Disabled no special facilities
Pets accepted
Closed 4th Jan to 6th Feb
Proprietors Tim and Zara Whitmore

The South-West

Spa town hotel, Eugénie-les-Bains (Landes)

Le Couvent aux Herbes

In an elegant little spa town – which became fashionable under the Second Empire – dominated by the activities of her well-known husband, Michel Guérard, this charming hotel is where Mme Guérard displays her talents for decoration and hospitality. A beautiful 18thC building, it was recently a girls' boarding school. At the inspiration of Mme Guérard, it was transformed into the ultimate in gracious living, with only eight rooms and suites. Each is different in furnishing and decoration and infinite care is lavished on every detail. Rooms have names heavy with nostalgia; the *Jardin Secret* opens on to a herb garden. Steps lead down from the convent to the colonial grandeur of the larger hotel, Les Prés d'Eugénie, where the renowned cuisine of the master chef, Michel Guérard, can be savoured, as only breakfast is served at the smaller hotel. This is a place for those wanting to spoil themselves in an atmosphere of luxury and refinement and prepared to pay for it. All the buildings in the Guérard complex are in parklike surroundings and guests are free to move from one to the other. M Guérard is very keen on simplicity; this is the simple life at a premium, but nonetheless charming. Sister hotel to La Maison Rose, page 63.
Nearby Aire-sur-Adair; Mont-de-Marsan.

40320 Eugénie-les-Bains
Tel 05 58 05 06 07
Fax 05 58 51 10 10
Location in the Michel Guérard complex in the town
Meals breakfast only; other meals next door in Les Prés d'Eugénie
Prices FFFF
Rooms 8 double; all with bath, phone, TV, heating, hairdryer
Facilities swimming-pool, park, spa, parking
Credit cards all major
Children accepted
Disabled possible
Pets dogs accepted; 150F a day
Closed Dec to mid Feb
Proprietor M Guérard

The South-West

Spa town hotel, Eugénie-les-Bains (Landes)

La Maison Rose

The Empress Eugénie brought fame and fortune to this elegant little spa town in the 19thC when she came to take the waters. More recently, it has become associated with the name of chef Michel Guérard, creator of *cuisine minceur*; his Prés d'Eugénie in the large spa and leisure complex is one of the finest restaurants in France. Intended principally for guests taking a cure and requiring more modest accomodation than is elsewhere available in the town, this is a delightful place. Designed and decorated by Mme Guérard, it is light and airy and enlivened by brightly coloured furnishings and feels more like home than a hotel. The food may not be quite like home: meals here are for those watching their weight. Cooking courses are available, but for those wanting to break out and have something more substantial, M Guérard's Ferme Aux Grives is just a few steps away, where reasonably priced superb country-style lunches and dinners are available. Rooms are comfortable and charmingly decorated, some in smart checks, with old tiles. More expensive suites include little 'old-fashioned' kitchens, with everything provided from electric coffee machines to steamer pans. Sister hotel to the Convent aux Herbes, page 62.

Nearby Mont-de-Marsan; Pau (50km).

40320 Eugénie-les-Bains
Tel 05 58 05 05 05
Fax 05 58 51 13 59
Location in spa town
Meals all
Prices FF
Rooms 27 doubles, and 5 suites; all with bath, phone, TV, heating and hairdryer
Facilities swimming-pool, tennis courts, sauna, health centre, parking
Credit cards AE, MC, V
Children accepted
Disabled possible
Pets 1 dog only; 50F a day
Closed December
Proprietor M Guérard

The South-West

Riverside hotel, Grenade-sur-l'Adour (Landes)

Pain Adour et Fantaisie

Owner and chef Philippe Garret (he has a Michelin star) recently took over from Didier Oudill – now at the Café de Paris, Biarritz – under whom he had worked since the creation of this distinguished hotel/restaurant. Both served under Michel Guérard at Eugénie-les-Bains and this tutelage is evident as much in the standards of taste and quality in the design and furnishings of the rooms as in the refinement and authority of the cuisine and service. One half of the building was an 18thC *maison de maître* and has a superb stone staircase and fine oak panelling and carved fireplace in part of the dining-room. The other half is 17thC, with original arcading on to the market square and half-timbered walls. Much care has gone into selecting appropriate antique furniture and the atmosphere is enhanced with original paintings and fine mirrors. On the south side is a handsome wide terrace overhanging the river: a very romantic setting for a summer's evening, with elegantly-laid tables and green and white parasols. Bedrooms are spacious and the best are furnished in a modern style and have views over the river and whirlpool baths. They have fanciful names – one is *Clair de Lune*. Food is first-class.

Nearby Pau (50 km); Mont-de-Marsan (14 km); Biarritz.

7, place des Tilleuls
40270 Grenade-sur-l'Adour
Tel 05 58 45 18 80
Fax 05 58 45 16 57
Location on the river Adour
Meals all
Prices FF
Rooms 11 double; all with bath, shower, phone, TV, heating, hairdryer; some with air-conditioning, minibar, safe, whirlpool bath
Facilities terrace; garage 50F
Credit cards AE, DC, MC, V
Children accepted
Disabled 1 ground-floor room
Pets dogs; 50F a day
Closed never
Proprietor Philippe Garret

The South-West

Country hotel, Lacabarède (Tarn)

Demeure de Flore

This small hotel in the foothills of the mountains of the Haut-Languedoc was opened in 1992 by Monike and Jean-Marie Tronc – with 30 years of the business behind him – to realize their dream of a perfect hotel.

The 19thC *maison de maître* may be an undistinguished building, but it sits prettily in a mature, wooded *jardin anglais,* far enough from the passing RN112 to feel quite secluded. And, within, there is a delightful ambience. Stylish floral prints are set against warm, plain backgrounds. The house is full of floor-to-ceiling windows and the general impression is light and fresh. Carefully chosen antiques and ornaments give the feel of a lived-in but cared-for family home. The eight bedrooms are individually furnished in the same careful way. But for some it may be just a tiny bit too organized and planned to be charming. A recent guest told us he felt slightly uneasy about the squeaky-clean, Swiss-watch precision, everything-in-order aspect of the hotel and peculiarly wanted to subvert the tidiness of it all in some way. In a small hotel like this, does one really need plastic liners in the outside rubbish bins? Reports, please.

Nearby Castres (35 km); Albi (60 km); Toulouse (100 km).

106 Route Nationale
81240 Lacabarède
Tel 05 63 98 32 32
Fax 05 63 98 47 56
Location opposite service station on outskirts of village on RN112 between St-Pons and Mazamet; in gardens with ample parking
Meals all
Prices FF
Rooms 10 double, 1 suite; all with bath; all rooms have phone, TV, heating, hairdryer
Facilities sitting-room; dining-room; swimming-pool
Credit card MC, V
Children accepted
Disabled 1 room
Pets only by special arrangement; 70F a day
Closed open all year for reservations
Proprietors M and Mme Tronc

The South-West

Lakeside hotel, Mimizan (Landes)

Au Bon Coin du Lac

We are happy to report that we continue to see no sign of slippage in the high standards of Jean-Pierre Caule, the third generation of his family to run Au Bon Coin, or, indeed, the exacting standards of Mme Caule, who oversees things front of house. There is no pretence here – everything is genuine and it starts with the smile with which Mme greets you on arrival – it clearly comes from within.

Beside a large freshwater lake away from the noise and bustle of the seaside town, the hotel is a refuge of calm and repose, yet less than a kilometre from the sandy dunes and beaches for which this region is known. It is the gastronomic Mecca for this part of the Landes and amply justifies its reputation. Our inspector's dinner was a 'delight of refined dishes of an individuality not without surprises'. M Caule, who has a Michelin star, buys his own fish in nearby Arcachon. The dining-room is light and welcoming, with a terrace outside shaded by trees and awning, all looking over a smooth green lawn to the water, rowing boats and ducks. Bedrooms are unobtrusively furnished, cosy and restful. This is ideal for those who want four-star treatment, a relaxed and friendly atmosphere and excellent food.

Nearby Bordeaux (98 km); Arcachon (65 km); Dax (70 km).

34, avenue du Lac
40200 Mimizan
Tel 05 58 09 01 55
Fax 05 58 09 40 84
Location on edge of lake with garden; 2km N of Mimizan
Meals all
Prices FF
Rooms 4 double, all with bath and shower; 4 suites, all with bath and shower; all rooms have phone, TV, heating, fridge and hairdryer
Facilities sitting-room; terrace
Credit cards AE, MC, V
Children accepted
Disabled ground floor bedrooms
Pets not accepted
Closed never
Proprietors M and Mme Caule

The South-West

Riverside hotel, St-Étienne-de-Baïgorry (Pyrénées-Atlantiques)

Arcé

The setting – by a fast-flowing stream in a Basque village surrounded by mountains – is magical, best appreciated from the dining terrace, which juts out over the water and is sheltered by a canopy of chestnut trees. The food is almost as good as the view, featuring plenty of local specialities (game, fish), though Michelin withdrew its star a year or two ago. With such civilized treatment and accomodation, it is not suprising that it is high on the calling-list of international travellers. The Arcé family (they have been running this riverside enterprise since 1865) are more than equal to their mission and have no complacency about their success. Inside the shuttered building are spacious public rooms – a beamed sitting-room with brick fireplace, a library with books in all languages, and a smart dining-room with picture windows and a veranda by the river. Some bedrooms in a separate building have balconies overlooking the water. Green, white and red colours of the basque country predominate. Across a wooden bridge over the stream is a swimming-pool. It is a delightful and excellent base for excursions on foot or by car into the mountains of Spain and the surrounding area.

Nearby walking, fishing, cycling; Pyrenees; Atlantic coast.

64430 St-Étienne-de-Baïgorry
Tel 05 59 37 40 14
Fax 05 59 37 40 27
Location in village 10 km W of St-Jean-Pied-de-Port
Meals all
Prices FF
Rooms 22 double, 1 single; all with phone, TV, heating and hairdryer
Facilities swimming-pool; sitting-rooms; games-room; library; tennis court; garden; car parking
Credit cards DC, MC, V
Children accepted
Disabled no facilities
Pets Accepted
Closed mid-Nov to mid-March
Proprietor M Arcé

Village inn, St-Félix-Lauragais (Haute-Garonne)

Auberge du Poids Public

This modest original village inn takes its name from the old-fashioned weighbridge outside and is now eclipsed by a superb restaurant. The owner/chef, Claude Taffarello, (one Michelin star) started as an apprentice in the kitchens here and after years spent gathering experience elsewhere returned to take over in 1990. The main inside dining-room is rustic in decoration, with oak-beamed walls and ceilings, flagged floor, and old domestic household objects on show (bottles, flat irons, weights and measures); a large window looks over gently rolling farmland. Another dining-room opens on to a chic, elegant terrace, with colonial tent-style parasols, pink and white table-cloths and chairs with pink-and-grey striped cushions. Service is impeccable and highly professional, food excellent and it is not surprising that it is treated as something of a place of pilgrimage, with people coming from afar. (Our inspector watched trays of *ceps* being delivered and felt they looked really too good to eat and should be used instead to illustrate coffee-table cookbooks.) Bedrooms are being gradually updated from good *auberge* standard, but they are secondary to what goes on downstairs in the kitchen.

Nearby Castres (36 km); Toulouse (42 km).

31540 St-Felix-Lauragais
Tel 05 61 83 00 20
Fax 05 61 83 86 21
Location in middle of village at junction of D622 and D20
Meals all
Prices F
Rooms 13 double; 9 with bath, 4 with shower; all with phone, TV, heating, minibar; 2 with hairdryer
Facilities dining-room; terrace; boutique; car parking
Credit cards AE, CB, MC, V
Children accepted
Disabled no facilities
Pets accepted
Closed Jan
Proprietor Claude Taffarello

The South-West

Seaside town hotel, St-Jean-de-Luz (Pyrénées-Atlantiques)

Hotel Parc Victoria

The owner – once a neighbour – of this gleaming white 19thC villa rescued it from demolition and spent four years restoring the house and garden to their former glory. The place is now immaculate; the predominant feeling is of space, light and colour, both inside and out. The park that gives the house its name has neat lawns, formal flower beds and magnificent mature cedars and pines. M Larralde scoured antique shops to find furnishings and fittings to make his dream come true and the hotel is filled with charming pieces. The elegant *salon* of the main house is in the Napoléon III style, complete with chandeliers. Bedrooms are luxurious with marble bathrooms. Some rooms have their own balconies; some suites have their own small gardens. There is a very attractive and successful addition alongside the generous terrace of the swimming-pool which provides a veranda-style dining-room and relaxation area with sunbeds and exercise equipment. All is white, enlivened by blue and the Basque colours of red and green. Lunch can be served by the pool and tea on the terrace. Our reporter was most impressed by 'service and food of the highest standard'.

Nearby St-Jean-de-Luz; Spanish border, Biarritz (16 km).

5 rue Cepé
64500 St-Jean-de-Luz
Tel 05 59 26 78 78
Fax 05 59 26 78 08
Location 2 km from town centre in Quartier du Lac
Meals all
Prices FFF-FFFF
Rooms 10 double, 2 suites; all with bath, shower, phone, TV, heating, minibar, hairdryer
Facilities park, swimming-pool, sea 200 metres
Credit cards AE, DC, V
Children accepted
Disabled 1 room
Pets dogs accepted; 60F a day
Closed 15th Nov to 15th March
Proprietor M Larralde

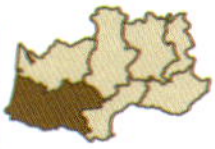

The South-West

Village hotel, Sare (Pyrénées-Atlantiques)

Hôtel Arraya

With its timbered, white-painted houses, Sare can claim to be the prettiest of all the extremely pretty Basque villages. In the heart of the village, this 17thC house was once an overnight resting place for pilgrims on their way across the Pyrenees to Santiago de Compostela. Behind the slightly severe frontage on the main square lies a country-style hotel of great character, now run by the third generation of the Fagoago family. It is very clean, airy and light, with much old, dark, burnished wood. The beamed sitting-room and dining-room – and every nook and cranny on stairways and landings – are filled with glorious old Basque furniture; sofas and chairs are comfortable and inviting and flowers are everywhere.

The bedrooms are most attractive (some border on the small, however) with colourful bedspreads made by a member of the Fagoago family. Some look out over the splendidly verdant garden; others have a view of the village square. There's a handsome, curved wooden staircase to the upper floor. Summer eating is done on the terrace; the cooking is good, with regional dishes a speciality of the house and there's a particularly well-chosen wine list.
Nearby Aïnhoa (10 km); St-Jean-de-Luz (14 km); Biarritz (29 km).

64310 Sare
Tel 05 59 54 20 46
Fax 05 59 54 27 04
Location in middle of village, 14 km SE of St-Jean-de-Luz
Meals all
Prices F-FF
Rooms 21; 20 double, 1 single; 16 with bath, 5 with shower; all with phone, TV, heating and hairdryer
Facilities garden; terrace; parking
Credit cards AE, MC, V
Children accepted
Disabled ground-floor rooms
Pets no
Closed mid-Nov to mid-April
Proprietor M Paul Fagoaga

The South-West

Riverside hotel, Sauveterre-de-Béarn (Pyrénées-Atlantiques)

Hôtel du Vieux Pont

The setting is breathtaking; the hotel sits on medieval arches on the bank of one the best salmon rivers in France, the Gave d'Oloron, next to a ruined bridge which is the stuff of legends. Above is the ruined castle and other remains of old Sauveterre. The veranda of the hotel opens on to all this – floodlit at night – and to sit there having a drink or an evening meal can be most romantic.

Two British former journalists, Paul and Sandie Williams, have entirely renovated the once abandoned hotel – to great effect. All the bedrooms are light and attractively finished; some have balconies. Those on the top floor are under a mansard roof. There's an indoor dining-room and well-appointed kitchen on the ground floor, leading on to the terrace overlooking the fast-flowing river. The food here is 'international', and the menu is limited but imaginative. The hotel is completely secluded, out of sight or sound of the town, and the hosts extend a warm welcome to guests. The accent is on informality. Parking, though, can be tricky; access is by a steepish narrow road and, to get out again, is best tackled in reverse. Help is at hand for drivers who can't face it.

Nearby Orthez; Dax; the Pyrenees; Atlantic coast.

Rue du Pont de la Légende
64390 Sauveterre-de-Béarn
Tel 05 59 38 95 11
Fax 05 59 38 99 10
Location on river's edge in historic town; turn off RN113 to Pont de la Légende
Meals all
Prices F
Rooms 5 double and 2 family suites; 1 with twin beds; all with bath, phone, TV, heating and hairdryer
Facilities terrace; fishing
Credit cards MC, V
Children accepted
Disabled no facilities
Pets accepted
Closed 1st Nov to mid-March
Proprietors Paul and Sandie Williams

Languedoc-Roussillon

Country hotel, Céret (Pyrénées-Orientales)

Le Mas Trilles

Laszlo Bukk is a Lithuanian-born, Swiss-trained experienced (including spells in Canada and Australia) hotelier and his Breton wife has extended her artistic and design talents into the world of very refined cuisine. In a labour of love, they have transformed this 17thC *mas* into a delightful welcoming hotel – blending past and present and endowing it with their own very personal presence and aura. The massive warm stone structure overlooks the fast-flowing River Tech – a tiny path brings you down to a stretch between two bends where the clear water looks almost still – an unspoiled natural sanctuary. A terrace beside the house leads down to a delightfully uncomplicated garden with lawn and swimming-pool, ancient trees and flowering shrubs. Rooms are practical, immaculate and all have either a terrace or a small private garden: nothing formal or stiff and guests feel relaxed enough to acknowledge one another if they are so inclined. The menu for dinner is chalked up on a board and this gives those with special requirements the opportunity to ask for something different. But few are likely to as the kitchen is Mme Bukk's passion and pride – and rightly so. Superb food.

Nearby Perpignan; beaches (30km).

Le Pont de Reynes
66400 Céret
Tel 04 68 87 38 37
Fax 04 68 87 42 62
Location in countryside; on D115 2 km from Céret
Meals breakfast, demi-pension dinner (obligatory during season)
Prices FF-FFF
Rooms 10 double; all with bath, shower, phone, TV, heating
Facilities heated pool; garden; table tennis; locked parking
Credit cards MC, V
Children accepted
Disabled 1 room
Pets accepted; 50F a day
Closed mid-Oct to Easter
Proprietors M and Mme Bukk

Languedoc-Roussillon

Country hotel, Céret (Pyrénées-Orientales)

La Terrasse au Soleil

The original part of the hotel was an 18thC *mas* but already a hotel when the present owners acquired it in 1980. Since then two annexes have been added for extra bedrooms and suites. The setting is lovely, higher up the mountains than nearby Céret, with splendid views over unspoiled hills.

Bedrooms vary in size, but the biggest are very spacious and all are tastefully furnished and decorated (some have their own private verandas). There is plenty of individuality in the interior design – much of it the legacy of Charles Trenet (the house at one time belonged to his agent and was a haunt of show-business personalities): unusual terracotta and ceramic tiling and imported African wood carvings, as in the huge bar. Colour and warmth in abundance introduce intimacy and cosiness not normally found in four-star hotels. Picasso is said to have sat on the terrace to enjoy the views of Mont Canigou.

The restaurant, La Cerisaie, has a very high reputation and a new 24-year-old chef from Paris. At lunchtime, there is a tempting *carte brasserie* as a lighter alternative to the more serious food served at dinner.

Nearby Perpignan; beaches (30km).

Route de Fontfrède
66400 Céret
Tel 04 68 87 01 94
Fax 04 68 87 39 24
Location in Pyrenean foothills above town, 26 km SW of Perpignan; with gardens and parking
Meals all
Prices FFF-FFFF
Rooms 25 double; all with bath; air-conditioning, phone, TV, minibar, hairdryer
Facilities heated pool; tennis court (floodlit); golf practice; children's garden; helipad
Credit cards AE, MC, V
Children accepted
Disabled 3 ground-floor rooms
Pets accepted if well-behaved
Closed 1st Nov to end Feb
Proprietors M and Mme Leveille-Nizerolle

Languedoc-Roussillon

Seaside town hotel, Collioure (Pyrénées-Orientales)

Hôtel Casa Païral

Tucked away in a small *impasse*, it is magical to find this quiet, elegant hotel just 150 yards from the busiest part of Collioure, close to the harbour and main beach with their many seaside cafés, restaurants, and narrow packed streets winding up the hill. A period-piece Catalan-style house built in the mid-19thC, it has a lush, picturesque interior garden with 100-year-old palm trees and pines shading a courtyard with tables and chairs and (somewhat apart) a swimming-pool. The attractive ground-floor *salon* has a tiled floor and looks out to the courtyard and a fountain backed by oleanders and a huge magnolia. There is also a larger 1930s-style *salon* with TV and card table. The breakfast room (down a stone staircase) is captivating – and surprising; in one corner is the trunk of a vast oak tree which grows out through the roof, while opposite large windows frame beautiful views of the garden. Bedrooms in the main house combine old-world charm in the sleeping area with modern bathroom facilities. Our inspector was overcome by nostalgia: 'It reminded me of how good hotels used to be, but with all mod cons. A place full of charm.'

Nearby Port-Vendres (4 km); Perpignan (27 km); Argelès-sur-Mer (6.5km).

66190 Collioure
Tel 04 68 82 05 81
Fax 04 68 82 52 10
Location in centre of seaside town; 150 m from port and beach; with locked private parking (40F)
Meals breakfast only
Prices FF
Rooms 28 double; 24 with bath, 4 with shower; all with phone, TV, heating, minibar; 9 rooms have air-conditioning; hairdryer on request
Facilities swimming-pool; secure parking; secluded garden
Credit cards all
Children accepted
Disabled some ground-floor rooms
Pets accepted; 30F a day
Closed 1st Nov to mid-March
Director Mme de Bon

Languedoc-Roussillon

Hilltop village hotel, Cornillon (Gard)

La Vieille Fontaine

Built within the walls of the ruined château of a medieval fortified village, with cobbled streets and ivy-clad ramparts, this little hotel is full of charm. *Patron* and chef, M Audibert, is a Marseillais; his *gratinée de langoustines* and *chou farci à la provençale,* accompanied by the local Tavel *rosé,* have long been the restaurant's attractions. The hotel is the creation of Mme Audibert, a native of this once semi-abandoned village. Inspired by the Louvre pyramid, she has, with great flair, clad the exterior circular staircase to the bedrooms with an elegant glass structure, at which one can gaze in wonder over breakfast in the courtyard.

Her decorating style is simple and pretty; tiled bathrooms, Provençal fabrics, furniture from local *antiquaires.* One room contains a great chunk of the old château wall. Most have terraces; numbers 7 and 8 have views way over the top of the castle wall to the south. A steep flight of stone steps through terraced gardens leads to the pool. Water gushing in from the hillside creates the illusion that you are bathing in a mountain stream.

The welcome is spontaneous and warm; dinner on the terrace looking over the hills and vineyards of the Gard is a delight.

Nearby Orange; Avignon; the Gorges of the Ardèche.

30630 Cornillon
Tel 04 66 82 20 56
Fax 04 66 82 33 64
Location well into the village, with limited vehicular access
Meals all
Prices FF-FFF
Rooms 8 double; all with bath and shower, TV, phone, electric heating, and entrance hall; 6 with terraces
Facilities pool; terraced garden; sitting-room; dining-room; courtyard; terrace
Credit cards all except DC
Children welcome
Disabled not possible
Pets accepted: 55F a day
Closed Jan and Feb
Proprietors M and Mme Audibert

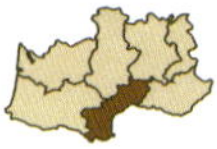

Languedoc-Roussillon

Village hotel, Gincla (Aude)

Hostellerie du Grand Duc

The Grand Duc is the eagle owl, presiding (stuffed) over the fire-place in the beamed dining-room of this delightful, modest little Logis. A refurbished 18thC *maison de maître* (the *maître* made his living from the surrounding forests), it was opened 12 years ago as a restaurant by the son of the Bruchet family, a chef, whose father is a wine inspector from Burgundy. The wide central hallway has original stone walls and the fine old staircase has terracotta tiles with oak nosings and wrought iron balustrade. There's a large dining-room and a superb modern kitchen with the latest German electronic oven, where they make their own bread.

The bedrooms are large, but somewhat disappointing with fussy wallpaper, which comes as an aesthetic let-down after the nice, clean lines of the dining-room, with its whitewashed walls. Admirers return year after year to write flattering remarks in the visitors' book: 'Gets better all the time – everything, reception, service, food and comfort is excellent'. Our inspector – wallpaper excepted – found it charming. There's a pleasant terrace, looking on to a fountain and old lime trees; in summer you dine outside by candle light.

Nearby Perpignan (63km); Quillan (23km); Forêt de Fanges.

2, route de Boucheville
11140 Gincla
Tel 04 68 20 55 02
Fax 04 68 20 61 22
Location in a small village 63 km NW of Perpignan
Meals all
Prices F
Rooms 8 double and 1 family suite; 5 with bath, 4 with shower; all with phone, TV, heating, hairdryer
Facilities terrace; parking; forest walks
Credit cards MC, V
Children accepted
Disabled no special facilities
Pets accepted
Closed 15th Nov to 15th March
Proprietors M and Mme Bruchet

Languedoc-Roussillon

Village inn, Llo (Pyrénées-Orientales)

Auberge Atalaya

A charming small hotel in superb unspoiled mountain country had our inspector enraptured: 'Magic'. The little village of Llo straggles up the mountainside, its stone buildings imperceptibly blending into the rock. The Catalan-speaking Cerdagne is half in Spain and half in France and no-one quite knows where or when. The Atalaya itself appears to be growing out of the crag on either side of a mountain road and is easily missed. Ingeniously sculpted, it is enchanting, built out of the materials of a ruined *mas* so as to be entirely in harmony with its natural surroundings. The distinguished cultured atmosphere inside emanates from the personality and taste of M and Mme Toussaint (his mother earned official praise from the British government for helping Allied escapees cross into neutral Spain). There is a serenity and humanity which spreads a warmth that is welcoming without being in the least intrusive. Warmth is also found in the antique furniture and tasteful fabrics which give the natural feel of a home rather than a showroom. The terrace has corners, where one can be very private, and views everywhere that are expansive and uplifting. Good food adds to the exhilarating sense of being on top of the world.
Nearby Odeillo (10 km); Ront-Romeu (15 km).

66800 Llo
Tel 04 68 04 70 04
Fax 04 68 04 01 29
Location in middle small village, 2 km E of Saillagouse and 10 km E of Bourg-Madame; ample parking
Meals all
Prices FF
Rooms 12 double, 1 suite; 10 with bath; 3 with shower; all with phone, TV, heating, minibar, safe; hairdryer on request
Facilities sitting-room; bar; dining-room; swimming-pool; terrace
Credit cards MC, V
Children accepted
Disabled no facilities
Pets accepted
Closed 5th Nov to 2th Dec
Proprietors M and Mme Toussaint

Château hotel, Madières (Hérault)

Château de Madières

'Exceptionally excellent' enthused our inspector, after visiting this 14thC fortress, perched above the Vis river gorge and rescued from decay in the mid-1980s by the present owners. After a career in fashion design in Paris, Mme Brucy transferred her artistic talent and expertise to more durable materials and, with her husband, has created a remarkably successful and exciting blend of ancient and modern beauty. Comfortable rooms have been made within the existing framework of medieval walls and arches, with no loss to the historic feel of the place. No two bedrooms are alike; there's luxury and light and colour in abundance. All have modern bathrooms. The best are spacious and delightfully furnished, with bold colourful fabrics against white walls and oriental rugs on tiled floors. The public rooms are superb. The galleried sitting-room has a vast Renaissance fireplace. The vaulted dining-room, jutting out of the main building and with a terrace above, has spectacular views across the gorge through arched windows. A courtyard leads to a swimming-pool with fitness room and terraces go down to the river below. Excellent food; an ideal place to relax the mind and body; warm welcome.

Nearby Cirque de Navacalles; Grottes des Demoiselles; Ganges.

Madières
34190 Ganges
Tel 04 67 73 84 03
Fax 04 67 73 55 71
Location on hillside overlooking village, on crossroads of D48 and D25; with large grounds and car parking
Meals all
Prices FFF-FFFF
Rooms 8 doubles and 4 suites; 5 rooms and all suites with bath; all with phone, sat TV, heating, minibar, hairdryer
Facilities 3 sitting-rooms; 2 dining-rooms; 3 terraces; heated pool; fitness room; table tennis
Credit cards all
Children if well-behaved
Disabled no facilities
Pets accepted
Closed most of Nov to March
Proprietors M and Mme Brucy

Languedoc-Roussillon

Village hotel, Minerve (Hérault)

Relais Chantovent

Minerve, an old Cathar refuge, is that rare thing – a 14thC fortified hilltop town unspoiled, as yet, by the tourist business. Tourists there are, but the industry has not yet taken over and the small town continues to have an ongoing organic life which is very appealing. With only two narrow streets up and down, cars have to be left below. It is no effort (except for the handicapped) and well worth the inconvenience.

The hotel is really in three parts, each equally attractive. There is a restaurant and stunning terrace looking across a deep gorge to a layered limestone cliff populated by birds and with vineyards on the top level. Then there's a separate building with bedrooms and, around the corner in the next street, an old village house, restored with care and charm, with sitting-room and fireplace, furnished in period harmony.

All the decoration is done with infinite attention to detail, but without fuss – light walls, uncluttered, attractive etchings and paintings. The Evenous – he is a Breton and an expert in preparing abundant local produce for the table – are a totally dedicated couple, with taste and finesse and a real love for what is their home.
Nearby Carcassonne (45 km); Narbonne (32 km); St-Pons (29 km).

17 Grande Rue
34210 Minerve
Tel 04 68 91 14 18
Fax 04 68 91 81 99
Location in small historic town 45 km NW of Carcassonne, with no vehicular access
Meals all
Prices F
Rooms 10 double; only 1 with bath, rest with shower; all with heating; hairdryer on request
Facilities public swimming-pool; terrace with splendid views
Credit cards MC, V
Children accepted
Disabled not suitable
Pets accepted
Closed 15th Dec to 15th Jan
Proprietors M and Mme Evenou

Languedoc-Roussillon

Country hotel, Olargues (Hérault)

Domaine de Rieumégé

In a lovely, natural setting of hills, rock, water, trees, shrubs and soft green grass, this sensitively restored 17thC stone house is in the middle of the Haut Languedoc national park and close to Olargues, one of the villages classed as the most beautiful in France. It is a perfect place for a stroll after dinner or before breakfast. There are few hotels in this area and although there is a road nearby, little traffic noise filters through. Deep, restful calm prevails. The attractive high-ceilinged beamed restaurant retains, even after restoration, its country barn origins. (The food our inspector had was excellent; the 'pleasant, not-too-professional service' was also much appreciated).

Bedrooms are simply furnished with respectable antique pieces – and comfortable. The beamed sitting-room, with open fire in cooler weather and oil-lamps, is cosy, with some handsome antique furniture. A smaller separate building has been adapted to provide a luxury room and suite, complete with its own garden and private swimming-pool. There is a wide range of accomodation here; three categories offer 'comfort', 'superior' and 'prestige', so there is something for all pockets.

Nearby Olargues (3 km).

Route de St-Pons
34390 Olargues
Tel 04 67 97 73 99
Fax 05 67 97 78 52
Location in countryside, 3 km from Olargues
Meals all
Prices FF-FFFF
Rooms 10 doubles, 3 family, 1 suite; most with bath; all with phone, heating; TV on request
Facilities swimming-pool, tennis court; 14-hectare walled estate; parking
Credit cards AE, MC, V
Children accepted
Disabled no facilities
Pets clean and well-behaved ones accepted; 40F a day
Closed mid to Oct to Easter
Proprietors M and Mme Sylva

Languedoc-Roussillon

Converted mill, Ornaisons (Aude)

Le Relais du Val d'Orbieu

This hotel has been cleverly designed to provide everything which the overnight traveller or long-stay holidaymaker could wish for – made to measure. Extensions with red-tiled roofs have been added to the original old mill to form an integrated complex of rooms and suites, four sides of which enclose a verdant cloister of calm and privacy. Rooms are bright and modern – 15 have their own terrace. The choice of accomodation is particularly flexible for families with children. Although parts of the hotel are old, there's no feeling of a museum but rather a highly efficient and comfortable hostelry. There is ample room for everyone in the spacious grounds. The swimming-pool is equally serious and professional and is flanked by impressive stands of oleander. The excellent cuisine – fish dishes are especially good – and wine cellar reflect the personal passion of the owner, M Gonzalvez, the son of a vigneron. Quite a number of English wine-merchants make this hotel their base to sample the wines of the Corbières. Another regular booking is by American cyclists who tour the region on two wheels. There's a full-time gardener and home-grown vegetables and herbs feature prominently on the menus.
Nearby Narbonne (14 km).

11200 Ornaisons
Tel 04 68 27 10 27
Fax 04 68 27 52 44
Location in a 2-hectare garden in countryside next to a vineyard
Meals all
Prices FF-FFF
Rooms 14 double and 6 family suites; all with bath, shower, phone, sat TV, heating, minibar, hairdryer
Facilities garden; swimming-pool; tennis; practice golf; table tennis
Credit cards all
Children accepted
Disabled 1 room
Pets accepted
Closed last week Nov to last week Jan
Proprietors M and Mme Gonzalvez

Languedoc-Roussillon

Town hotel, Villeneuve-lès-Avignon (Gard)

Hôtel de l'Atelier

For those who wish to enjoy the artistic delights of Avignon but can't stand crowds, this is the place to stay. Over the bridge, on the other side of the Rhône, this house built for a cardinal in the 16thC provides a perfect base for visiting, only ten minutes by bus or a 30F cab-ride from the centre of Avignon.

The proprietor, M Gounaud, and his wife fled Paris for the peace of the provinces and have created an oasis of calm just off the main street of this historic little town. Once in the garden it could be difficult to tear oneself away – even for Avignon. Immediately to the rear of this beautiful old house is a courtyard, where breakfast is served on little white tables under the shade of fig trees and a vine. And through a stone gateway, beyond, is another gloriously overgrown 'secret garden', a riot of oleander, geraniums and climbing roses in the early summer. Two of the rooms are actually *in* the garden and appealingly private. M Gounaud, who has a dog called Wagner, likes to be constantly on hand to give advice on where to go and what to see; there are Cezanne and Toulouse-Lautrec prints on the walls. In the afternoons, the dining-room turns into a *salon-de-thé*.

Nearby Avignon; Fort St-André; Chartreuse du Val de Bénédiction.

5, rue de la Foire
30400 Villeneuve-lès-Avignon
Tel 04 90 25 01 84
Fax 04 90 25 80 06
Location in the town
Meals breakfast only
Prices F-FF
Rooms 19; 11 with double bed, 8 twin; 13 with bath, 6 with shower; some with TV; all with phone, heating
Facilities sitting-rooms; garden
Credit cards all major
Children accepted
Disabled access difficult
Pets dogs welcome
Closed Nov
Proprietors M and Mme Gounaud

Auvergne & the Massif Cental

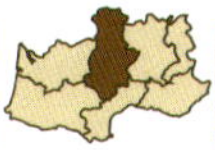

Manor house hotel, Castelpers (Aveyron)

Château de Castelpers

Yolande Tapié de Celeyron, of the old and distinguished family that owns this beautiful house, has recently handed over the reins to her daughter, Mme de Saint-Palais, after 30 years. Our inspector found it a 'real delight' to share their home full of memories and objects of continuous history. On the stairs is a portrait of Mme Tapié's great-grandfather, an '*intendant militaire*' of Napoléon. Her grandfather (an engineer who pioneered the building of dams to harness water power and whose car licence plate was 9) restored and built on to the remains of a 17thC mill at the end of the 19thC. The result is not a grandiose château but something more like an unspoiled country house, kept as it has matured and been lived in. It is full of fine old furniture and pictures. Many of the beds are four-posters.

The taste here is timeless; the charm effortless. The park is enchanting – tall trees shading a long green sward running between a river and a stream. There are swings for children. It is a 'peaceful, reflective, soothing, timeless place, happy to be just itself', in the words of our inspector. His dinner and wine was excellent. The inexpensive prices give added appeal.

Nearby Château du Bosc (10 km); Sauveterre-de-Rouergue (20 km).

Castelpers
12170 Léderques
Tel 05 65 69 22 61
Fax 05 65 69 25 31
Location in countryside 9 km SE of RN88, 10 km S of Naucelle; in wooded park with private car parking
Meals all – residents only
Prices F-FF
Rooms 8; 6 double, 1 with 2 double beds, 1 with double and single bed; 3 with bath, 5 with shower; all with phone; 4 with TV
Facilities sitting-room; 2 dining-rooms; park with chairs and tables under trees
Credit cards all
Children welcome if well-behaved
Disabled 1 ground-floor room
Pets accepted
Closed Oct to March
Proprietor Mme de Saint-Palais

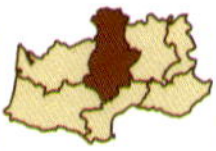

Auvergne & the Massif Cental

Village hotel, Conques (Aveyron)

Grand-Hôtel Sainte-Foy

Promotion to a full entry was long overdue for this delectable hotel in a lovely old village; as it is, we are somewhat behind the French tourist authorities, who in 1993 promoted the Sainte-Foy to four-star status – the first hotel in Aveyron to achieve the rating. Marie-France and Alain Garcenot, proprietors since they took over from an aunt in 1987, are justifiably proud of their achievement, but the facilities that are required for star-ratings are not the basis of the hotel's appeal.

Hôtel Sainte-Foy is a lovingly restored, partly timbered old house which takes its name from the great abbey church directly opposite. The house has been beautifully furnished with close attention to detail and to the character of the building. The warm glow of wood is everywhere. The large two-part sitting-room is particularly well furnished with antiques. Bedrooms are highly individual, tasteful and large, with views either over the church or the flowery courtyard garden.

You can dine here or in the intimate but pleasantly spacious rooms inside. The increasingly inventive cooking (daily changing menus) gets good reviews.

Nearby Church of Ste-Foy (remarkable tympanum and treasury).

Conques
12320 St-Cyprien-sur-Dourdou
Tel 05.65.69.84.03
Fax 05.65.72.81.04
Location in heart of village, 40 km N of Rodez; with private car parking
Meals breakfast, lunch, dinner
Prices F-FFF
Rooms 15 double, 2 suites, all with bath; all rooms have central heating, phone
Facilities 3 dining-rooms, sitting-room, bar, interior patio, conference room; 2 terraces; exercise room
Credit cards AE, MC, V
Children accepted
Disabled no special facilities
Pets accepted
Closed end Oct to Easter
Proprietors Marie-France and Alain Garcenot

Auvergne & the Massif Cental

Country hotel, Coulandon (Allier)

Le Chalet

Reviewing the entry of this Logis deep in the Bourbonnais countryside always raises an editorial smile, and not only because of the proprietor's name. We first visited it on a summer evening when its secluded, wooded garden (park-like in style and set out some 100 years ago) seemed idyllic. The big fish pond (where guests are welcome to fish) was perfect for strolling around, drink in hand, before pausing a while on the little raised terrace and then proceeding in to dinner.

It's a modest, traditional place. Rooms (in the chalet-style building itself, and in converted outbuildings) vary in style and size; none is notably stylish, but the best are cheerfully comfortable (with exposed beams and bright wallpaper).

Some interesting regional specialities are served in the traditional-style dining-room, and the service is amiable. Saint-Pourçain and Sancerre are special features of the wine list. In suitable weather, meals are served outside on the terrace, which has views of the countryside.

Nearby Moulins – timbered houses, cathedral; Souvigny's abbey; Balaine Arboretum; the oak forest of Tronçais; Romanesque churches.

03000 Coulandon
Tel 04.70.44.50.08
Fax 04.70.44.07.09
Location in countryside 6 km W of Moulins, off D945; with large grounds and ample car parking
Meals breakfast, lunch, dinner
Prices F-FF
Rooms 19 double, 5 with bath, 14 with shower (5 twin); 9 family rooms, 6 with bath, 3 with shower; all rooms have central heating, phone, TV
Facilities dining-room, sitting-room; fishing, swimming-pool
Credit cards AE, DC, MC, V
Children accepted
Disabled 6 ground-floor bedrooms
Pets accepted
Closed mid-Dec to end Jan
Proprietor M H Hulot

Auvergne & the Massif Cental

Manor house hotel, La Malène (Lozère)

Manoir de Montesquiou

Set dramatically between two sheer rockfaces in the Gorges du Tarn, this attractive family-run castle-like 15thC manor house provides history as well as excellent value for money. When Louis XIII ordered all rebel fortresses to be razed, the noble Montesquiou family saved their home by carrying out 'special favours' for the king, but worse indignities were to follow. A later fire destroyed part of the house and, during the Revolution, Gabriel de Montesquiou was imprisoned and his terrified wife hid herself in a cave; when she re-emerged she was blind.

Today, the house is having happier times. Heavily creepered, it has an inner courtyard and bedrooms in the turret, with stunning views. Larger ones have four-poster canopied beds and rich velvet upholsteries. There's much highly-polished dark furniture, which suits the surroundings, but it is an unassuming, comfortable hotel and guests are well looked after, with good humour and consideration, by owners M and Mme Guillenet, who have been running the place and providing tasty regional fare for 30 years.

'Good-sized rooms, good food, very good views', reports a contented reader.

Nearby river trips; fishing; bathing; Ste-Enimie (15 km).

48210 La Malène
Tel 04 66 48 51 12
Fax 04 66 48 50 47
Location small village in the Gorges of the Tarn
Meals all
Prices FF
Rooms 10 and 2 suites; mostly twin; 7 with bath, 5 with shower; all with phone, TV, heating; hairdryer on request
Facilities 2 terraces; private car parking
Credit cards DC, MC, V
Children accepted
Disabled no special facilities
Pets accepted; 35F a day
Closed Nov to March
Proprietors M and Mme Guillenet

Auvergne & the Massif Cental

Country hotel, Meyrueis (Lozère)

Château d'Ayres

The lovely, stone, mainly 18thC, white-shuttered château stands on the site of a 12thC Benedictine monastery, now in the heart of the Cévennes National Park and in its own beautiful wooded grounds, with mature sequoias and oaks. Inside it is extremely handsome, with walnut and chestnut panelling in some rooms, vaulted ceilings and a profusion of good antiques and pictures. Bedrooms are well-appointed, with elegant, traditional furniture and carved mouldings. Some of the larger rooms have interesting bathrooms – extended into round towers or elevated on a mezzanine. Staff are friendly and helpful. Food is excellent. Owner Mme de Montjou is in charge of the kitchen – helped by her son, Thibault – and they specialize in Languedoc cuisine using plenty of local produce. M de Montjou is a knowledgeable *sommelier.* The house has a relaxed and convivial atmosphere and is extremely quiet. The garden is superb, with a lake, tennis court, swimming-pool made out of local stone and a small whirlpool bath. There are plenty of alluring, shady places under the trees to which you can retreat with a chair and a book on long, hot afternoons – at 750 metres the air is wonderfully fresh and pure.

Nearby Meyrueis (1 km); Gorges du Tarn; Mont Aigoual (1,387 m).

48150 Meyrueis
Tel 04 66 45 60 10
Fax 04 66 45 62 26
Location on a wooded estate 1 km from Meyrueis
Meals all
Prices FF
Rooms 20 and 7 suites; 24 with bath, 3 with shower; all with phone, sat TV, heating, hairdryer
Facilities pool; terrace; library; tennis; car parking
Credit cards AE, DC, MC, V
Children accepted
Disabled no special facilities
Closed 15th Nov to end March
Proprietors M and Mme Montjou

Farmhouse hotel, Moudeyres (Haute-Loire)

Le Pré Bossu

Moudeyres is a remote village of thatched, stone cottages and farm buildings, high (1,200 m) in the volcanic Mézenc massif, surrounded by fields of wild flowers in the spring and mushrooms in the autumn. It is a long way off the beaten track, but our inspector found it well worth the journey: 'Rarely have I seen a more beautiful location, very *Wuthering Heights* and very difficult to get to.'

The conscientious Flemish owners, the Grootaerts, have worked extremely hard to create an attractive and comfortable house. To original beams, wooden floors and old-fashioned, open fireplaces, they've added antique dressers, lace curtains, wild flowers when they are available – dried flowers when they are not – and books. Pots of home-made jam and artisan products are (subtly) for sale.

Some of our reports suggest that there may be the occasional lack of warmth in the hospitality, while others enthuse over the comfort and the very high standard of the food (the kitchen has a Michelin star, which is a remarkable achievement). Bedrooms are appropriately rustic – clean and simple – and the whole place is fresh and well-kept. Picnic baskets are provided for lunching out. **Nearby** restored 18thC farm; Le Puy (25 km) – volcanic rock formations.

43150 Moudeyres
Tel 04 71 05 10 70
Fax 04 71 05 10 21
Location on edge of village, 25 km SE of Le Puy, beyond Laussonne; in garden with ample parking
Meals all
Prices F-FF
Rooms 10 double; 5 with bath, 5 with shower; all with heating, phone
Facilities TV room, dining-room
Credit cards AE, MC, V
Children accepted
Disabled no special facilities
Pets accepted (in bedrooms but not in dining-room)
Closed mid-Nov to Easter
Proprietor M Grootaert

Auvergne & the Massif Cental

Country hotel, Najac (Aveyron)

Longcol

This splendid turreted restored medieval farmhouse – with added buildings in the same bell-shaped slate-roofed style – is set in isolated grandeur in a forested valley of the Gorges de l'Aveyron.

Solid and dignified, the overall effect is most pleasing. Much skill and taste has gone into the architecture, fittings and furnishings and everywhere – in every room – there are antiques. Quite a few of the pieces are European, but mostly they are from Asia: huge carved and studded Indian doors, wood carvings and bronzes from India, Burma and Thailand, Indian miniature paintings on silk and ivory, all wonderfully exotic and cleverly lit and displayed. One could be in a luxury hotel in India. The Belgian owner, Mme Luyckx, began work on the site in 1982 with her mother (who died before completion) – she clearly has a passion for Asian art and antiques.

Added to all this is a sense of great comfort and professionalism. Seafood and regional dishes are served in a light and airy dining-room or on the little walled terrace in summer – or by the angular swimming-pool, which has views of woods. Food is taken seriously and there is an excellent wine list.

Nearby Najac (5 km); Cordes (30 km).

La Fouillade
12270 Najac
Tel 05 65 29 63 36
Fax 05 65 29 64 28
Location on D638, on large wooded estate NW of village, NE of Najac
Meals all
Prices FFF
Rooms 17 double; 15 with bath, 2 with shower; all with phone, TV, heating, minibar
Facilities pool; tennis; billiards (French); fishing; car parking; helipad
Credit cards AE, MC, V
Children accepted
Disabled no special facilities
Pets welcome
Closed 15th Nov to Easter
Proprietor Mme Fabienne Luyckx

Village hotel, Najac (Aveyron)

L'Oustal du Barry

This spick-and-span little *logis* – in the same family for five generations – is in one of the most beautiful villages in France.

Since the untimely accidental death in 1994 of her husband, Jean-Marie, Mme Miguel has assumed full responsibility for carrying on the tradition. This she does with skill, dedication and charm and her welcome is personal. The setting, overlooking a thickly wooded valley, is splendid. The dining-room, in country style, is spacious and has views of the garden; there is a terrace which is perfect for meals outside. Food is taken very seriously here. The kitchen facilities are as impressive as the air-conditioned wine cellar holding 12,000 bottles. It is a pretty sight to see kitchen staff out in the garden picking fresh herbs before lunch and it makes one want to hurry to the table. Meals are prepared and presented with delicacy and imagination.

Bedrooms vary. The best have terraces overlooking the valley or with views over rooftops to the castle of Najac. Mme Miguel has a programme under way to soften and lighten the interior decoration of the bedrooms. We were very taken with this traditional French country inn.

Nearby Villefranche-de-Rouergue (20 km); Cordes (30 km).

Place du Bourg
12270 Najac
Tel 05 65 29 74 32
Fax 05 65 29 75 32
Location in a fortified medieval village
Meals all
Prices F
Rooms 20 double; with bath or shower; all with phone, heating and hairdryer
Facilities garden; sitting areas; children's play area; secure car parking
Credit cards AE, MC, V
Children accepted
Disabled lift (5 floors)
Pets accepted
Closed 1st Nov to 1st April
Proprietor Mme Catherine Miguel

Auvergne & the Massif Cental

Village hotel, Plaisance (Aveyron)

Hostellerie Les Magnolias

This enchanting 17thC village house has very individual charm and character. It claims fame as having been the home of the brother of the French poet, Paul Valéry, who visited often and, seeing the splendid magnolias in the garden, gave it its name. Today, it is owned by chef Francis Roussel, from a long line of local masons and so perfectly suited both to preserve the fabric of the place and to develop a cuisine of note.

Redolent of history, the atmosphere is enhanced by respectable pieces of antique furniture and pictures in all the rooms. Bedrooms are simple, but comfortable. A fine old stone staircase, with wrought-iron rail, leads up to a dining-room, with beams, flagged floor and enormous open fireplace, looking out to a garden on the same level where one can see the famous magnolias, which are certainly 150 years old if not 300. Mme Roussel is charming and welcoming: she and her husband are dedicated to making this intriguing legacy live with hospitality and warmth. The food is where M Roussel puts most of his heart; he is passionate about the dishes he serves, made from fresh local home-grown produce and destined to become, perhaps, as celebrated as the magnolias.
Nearby Albi (40 km).

12550 Plaisance
Tel 05 65 99 77 34
Fax 05 65 94 70 57
Location just up the hill in Plaisance on D106
Meals all
Prices F
Rooms 6 double; 3 with bath, 3 with shower; all with phone, TV, heating and hairdryer
Facilities terrace
Credit cards all
Children accepted
Disabled not possible
Pets accepted; 25F a day
Closed Jan to March
Proprietor Francis Roussel

Riverside hotel, St-Jean-du-Bruel (Aveyron)

Hôtel du Midi-Papillon

Every year we receive a long hand-written bulletin from Jean-Michel Papillon, the fourth generation of Papillons to run this old coaching inn, reporting on the latest developments. Readers share our enthusiasm for the place, telling us that nothing changes, the food remains 'wonderful', the welcome 'faultless', the value 'outstanding'. Our inspector, to his pleasure, finds everything just so: 'The Papillons just go on doing what they have been doing for the last 150 years – providing a lively welcome, lodging and food to grateful travellers.' The hotel still bears features of its past and is the sort of traditional unpretentious *auberge* that is getting harder and harder to find; this one stands out for the quality of its food and the warmth of the welcome. There is an excellent dining-room – the domain of Mme Papillon – and a view from most tables of the river and a little medieval stone humpbacked bridge. There is also a terrace (though sometimes one may not always be able to sit where one wishes). Jean-Michel Papillon cooks with vegetables from the garden and home-raised poultry, and makes his own jam, croissants, and *charcuterie*. This is the rural, family-run inn at its best.

Nearby Gorges de la Dourbie (10 km); Montpellier-le-Vieux.

12230 St-Jean-de-Bruel
Tel 05 65 62 26 04
Fax 05 56 62 12 97
Location by river, in village, on D991, 40 km SE of Millau; with garden and garages
Meals all
Prices F
Rooms 18 doubles and 1 family suite; 13 with bath; all rooms have phone and heating
Facilities heated swimming-pool; whirlpool bath; sitting-room; TV room; fishing; country walks
Credit cards CB, MC, V
Children welcome
Disabled no special facilities
Pets accepted
Closed 11th Nov to Palm Sunday
Proprietors Maryse and Jean-Michel Papillon

Auvergne & the Massif Cental

Château hotel, Ydes (Cantal)

Château de Trancis

According to the brochure, if paradise existed it ought to resemble the Château de Trancis. But this originally rather ordinary Auvergnat *maison de maître,* transformed at the turn of the century into an Italian Renaissance château, bristling with turrets, may not be everyone's vision of heaven.

It is, however, owned and run with love and devotion by an English couple, Innes and Fiona Fennell (both former travel writers) who have brought to the enterprise great panache and dedication. (Restoration began in 1990; some of the shutters hadn't been opened for 40 years.) The style of decoration is grand and ornate; plenty of gilded mirrors, chandeliers, a Louis XIV *salon,* a 'German' dining-room and an 'English' library. Our inspector felt the whole was more a homage to a 19thC industrialist than to an aristocratic ideal. 'Apparently, the decoration appeals to the Europeans for its Englishness,' he noted, adding that the charm here lay very much in the Fennells' welcoming hospitality and that their eagerness and openness was even more impressive than the luxurious smartness of what they have created. Mrs Fennell cooks the five-course dinners.

Nearby Dordogne gorges; Parc Régional des Volcans d'Auvergne.

15210 Ydes
Tel 04 71 40 60 40
Fax 04 71 40 62 13
Location on D15, off D22, 2 km N of village of Saignes, 3 km E of Ydes; in countryside, with ample car parking
Meals breakfast; dinner
Prices FF-FFFF
Rooms 7 and 1 suite; 6 with bath, 2 with shower; all with heating, phone, sat TV, minibar, hairdryer
Facilities 3 sitting-rooms; 2 dining-rooms; 2 terraces; park; swimming-pool
Credit cards all
Children accepted
Disabled no special facilities
Pets not accepted
Closed mid-Oct to end Mar
Proprietors Innes and Fiona Fennell

Provence-Côte d'Azur

Country hotel, Aix-en-Provence (Bouches-du-Rhône)

Mas d'Entremont

This is one of our favourite hotels and a recent visit confirms our earlier impressions.(The hosts here are the charming M Marignane and his family – his brother owns the Relais de la Magdeleine at Gémenos, about which we are equally enthusiastic.) Low, red-roofed buildings are clustered around a courtyard – modern constructions, but using old materials. Within are wooden beams and pillars, rustic furniture, tiled floors and open fireplaces. Bedrooms are also rustic in style and comfortable. Many of the rooms are spread around the grounds in bungalows. The setting is peaceful and the gardens a delight – with a big swimming-pool shielded by cypresses, plenty of secluded corners, and a pond with a fountain, lilies and a decreasing number of lazy carp (a heron is under suspicion). Overlooking this is a beautiful summer dining-room, with windows that slide away, effectively creating a roofed terrace – to which underfloor heating has now been added, allowing you to eat out even on a chilly day.

The food is excellent, with the emphasis on fish, fresh vegetables and a strong Provençal influence (although the chef is from Strasbourg).

Nearby Aix-en-Provence; Abbaye de Silvacane (25 km).

Montée d'Avignon
13090 Aix-en-Provence
Tel 04 42 17 42 42
Fax 04 42 21 15 83
Location just off RN7, 2 km from centre of Aix, in large grounds
Meals all
Prices FFF
Rooms 15 doubles and 2 family; all with bath, shower, phone, heating, air-conditioning, minibar, sat TV, hairdryer, safe; terrace or balcony
Facilities pool; tennis; lift to 1st floor; car parking; terrace; large garden and grounds
Credit cards all except AE, DC
Children welcome
Disabled ground floor rooms and lift
Pets accepted
Closed 1st Nov to 15th March
Proprietors Marignane family

Provence-Côte d'Azur

Town hotel, Aix-en-Provence (Bouches-du-Rhône)

Hôtel des Quatre Dauphins

This attractive little 19thC *maison bourgeoise,* on a quiet corner near the pretty Place des 4 Dauphins, opened as a family-run hotel six years ago.

The dark-green front door sports four brass dolphins and bright red geraniums grow in window-boxes behind the wrought-iron bars on the ground floor. Built on three floors, there is no lift; it is simple, charming and excellent value for money. Some original features have remained – the lovely tiled terracotta floors – and there are some nice antique pieces throughout the house, such as handsome big mirrors, little wooden tables and a pine chest in the breakfast room. The plain décor in the rooms is very pleasing: walls are painted in pale pastel shades and bedspreads and curtains are in Provençal prints. Furniture is minimal, mainly painted wood. Bathrooms are well-equipped and spotless. Large, framed Impressionist posters hang in the corridors. The only public room is the breakfast/sitting-room, painted a gentle pale yellow, with large wooden painted Provençal-style armchairs, big ceramic pots, dried flowers and pretty table-cloths.

Perfect for visiting Aix on a budget.

Nearby Place des 4 Dauphins (50 m); Cours Mirabeau (100 m).

54 rue Roux Alphéron
13100 Aix-en-Provence
Tel 04 42 38 16 39
Fax 04 42 38 60 19
Location in town centre
Meals breakfast only
Prices F
Rooms 13; 12 double, 1 triple; 8 with bath, 5 with shower; all with phone, TV, heating, minibar
Facilities breakfast/sitting-room; public parking in street
Credit cards all except AE
Children welcome
Disabled not suitable
Pets small dogs accepted
Closed Feb (normally)
Proprietors M Juster and M Darricau

Provence-Côte d'Azur

Town villa, Aix-en-Provence (Bouches-du-Rhône)

Villa Gallici

The editor of our all-France guide considers the four-star Relais & Châteaux Villa Gallici to be the best hotel in Aix; a new inspection for this guide confirms its place at the top. (The restaurant, the Clos de la Violette, has a Michelin star.) It is certainly beautiful, and interior-designed down to the last curtain hook. Everything, inside and out, is perfect – gardens, terraces, pool, enormous terracotta pots overflowing with flowers, white umbrellas and plenty of wrought iron. A terrace, adjoining the villa, shaded by plane trees has been converted to an outside sitting-room with deep-cushioned sofas and chairs. Bedrooms are sumptuous, with marvellous French wallpapers and fabrics and elegant 18thC furniture. Bathrooms are often classic and pristine white. Downstairs, a series of small, welcoming, intimate sitting-rooms are filled with colour and light, prints, paintings, coffee-table books and pieces of porcelain. Our reporter noted that the guests were as beautiful as the hotel; this is not a place for the much-loved old grey T-shirt. Perhaps there is something just a little intimidating about the grand style of the Villa Gallici for it to be entirely relaxing, but that, as always, is a matter of taste.
Nearby Aix-en-Provence; Avignon (82 km); Marseille (31 km).

Avenue de la Violette
13100 Aix-en-Provence
Tel 04 42 23 29 23
Fax 04 42 96 30 45
Location in a quiet suburb, 500 m from cathedral, in extensive gardens; secure car parking
Meals all
Prices FFFF
Rooms 19 double; all with bath, phone, sat TV, heating, air-conditioning, minibar, video, hairdryer, safe
Facilities pool; garden
Credit cards all
Children welcome
Disabled 1 ground-floor room and bathroom
Pets welcome; 50F a day
Closed never
Proprietors M Jouve, M Dez and M Montemarco

Provence-Côte d'Azur

Country hotel, Auribeau (Alpes Maritimes)

Auberge de la Vignette Haute

This 'fantasy' hotel may not be everyone's idea of charming, but there are some charming corners of it. The original, unassuming hotel was destroyed by a forest fire which swept through Auribeau in 1986 and owner, M Meyer, has rebuilt it to make a personal dream come true. The result is extraordinary: a kind of neo-medieval theme-park. The house is of rustic stone, covered with creeper, with a dining terrace overlooking a swimming-pool designed along Roman-bath lines, with stone arches. Inside, all is medieval gloom. The lights are very low and you may well wonder where you are or where you are going. The dining-room, divided into three parts and lit by 400 oil lamps and candles, is a marvel. There are massive beams overhead, hayracks on the walls, pewter and wrought-iron objects everywhere and, in one section, a wall of glass separates diners from a little stable, where, knee-deep in straw, a donkey, a goat, a sheep and some rabbits gently munch their hay as you eat (well). Bedrooms are luxurious. Some are vaulted, others beamed; décor is, again, medieval with some very un-Middle-Ages touches such as whirlpool baths and, in one room, an electric bed. Staff are very proud of the place.
Nearby Grasse (9 km); Cannes (13 km).

06810 Auribeau-sur-Siagne
Tel 04 93 42 20 01
Fax 04 93 42 31 16
Location just outside village on the D509, 9 km SW of Grasse, with garden
Meals all
Prices FFFF
Rooms 12 double; all with bath, phone, sat TV, heating, air-conditioning, trouser press, hairdryer, safe
Facilities pool; dining-rooms; art gallery; farmyard; boules; parking
Credit cards all except DC
Children welcome; under-12s free
Disabled 1 room with special bath
Pets welcome; 70F a day
Closed never
Proprietor Jean-Jacques Meyer

Provence-Côte d'Azur

Country house, Ile de la Barthelasse (Vaucluse)

L'Anastasy

Staying with the Manguins on this green island just over the river from Avignon is as good as having friends with a house in Provence. Olga Manguin is an Italian who cooks like a dream and, indeed, out of season, holds cooking courses at L'Anastasy, an old farmhouse surrounded by orchards. The house has been restored with great style; there are long white curtains and plenty of comfortable sofas in the sitting-room. On the walls are pictures by the grandfather – a French fauvist painter – of Mme Manguin's husband, Henri. Guests sit together in the evenings – either at a big marble table in one of the two kitchens or out on the covered terrace – to eat whatever Mme Manguin has found in the market that day. Specialities of the house are home-made pasta and traditional dishes of Southern France, Italy and the Mediterranean, with olive oil, thyme, saffron and garlic. Bedrooms are basic; two are downstairs. They are spare rooms in a private house and do not pretend to be otherwise. The Manguins are seasoned and experienced hosts and the house has a welcoming, convivial air. All the attractions and bustle of Avignon are across the river; La Barthelasse, by contrast, is an island of tranquillity. Prices are a bargain.
Nearby Avignon; Aix-en-Provence.

Chemin des Poiriers
Ile de la Barthelasse
84000 Avignon
Tel 04 90 85 55 94
Fax 04 90 82 59 40
Location among fields and orchards
Meals breakfast and dinner
Prices F
Rooms 4; 1 with bath, 3 with shower
Facilities garden, terrace, swimming-pool, parking
Credit cards not accepted
Children accepted
Disabled no facilities
Pets accepted
Closed never
Proprietors M and Mme Manguin

Provence-Côte d'Azur

Country hotel, Les Baux-de-Provence (Bouches-du-Rhône)

Auberge de la Benvengudo

The Beaupied family's creeper-clad hotel, just outside the village of Les Baux, remains compelling – and much more affordable than most places in the area. Rooms have the style of a private country house: a cosy sitting-room with beams, an intimate dining-room and bedrooms with pretty patterned curtains. A surgeon came over to our inspector from the swimming-pool to say: "This is absolutely my idea of a charming small hotel. Just the place to spend a quiet, gentle relaxing week or 10 days. And the food is marvellous." Young Bocuse-trained chef Sebastien Beaupied has come home to manage the hotel for his parents – and, of course, to cook. Typical dishes are fresh monkfish with garlic and herbs and roast duckling with apples. The menu changes every day according to what is in the market. Although the garden adjoins the road, there are no complaints of noise. The bedrooms are in a separate building; some have balconies. A new building is planned as the friendly Benvengudo goes from strength to strength. The garden is delightful; there are olive groves and views of the natural stone outcrops of the Alpilles, the 'little Alps' of this part of Provence. Good walking country.

Nearby Les Baux-de-Provence village; St-Rémy-de-Provence; Arles.

Vallon de l'Arcoule
13520 Les Baux-de-Provence
Tel 04 90 54 32 54
Fax 04 90 54 42 58
Location outside the village of Les Baux-de-Provence on D78 to Fontvieille
Meals all
Prices FF-FFF
Rooms 20; 14 double, 6 twin; all with bath, phone, TV, heating, minibar; 12 with air-conditioning; 6 with terrace

Facilities pool, terrace, garden, tennis court, garages, secure car parking
Credit cards AE, MC, V
Children accepted
Disabled access possible
Pets dogs accepted; 55F a day
Closed 1st Nov to 1st Feb
Proprietors Beaupied family

Provence-Côte d'Azur

Village hotel, Bonnieux (Vaucluse)

L'Hostellerie du Prieuré

The crunch came for this attractive little hotel at the foot of the ramparts of one of the showpiece Luberon villages when it was left out of the Michelin guide for being devoid of *accueil* or welcome. Things have since changed, with the arrival of a new manager, Mme Contaz, who could not be more welcoming. A new chef, Gilles Lepoint, has come from Maxim in Paris to provide a Provençal table and Mme Contaz seems to be getting her own way with her desire to create a warm, relaxed ambience for guests. This former 18thC hospital – an *hôtel-Dieu* – has a splendid wide, red-tiled staircase leading up to the balustraded landing. (The former chapel is now used for storage.) What were once rooms for the patients are light and bright with antique furniture and spotless bathrooms, some of which have rough terracotta tiles. Some of the rooms overlook the pretty walled garden at the rear, where apricot and plum trees give shade from the heat, and are quieter than those at the front, which face the road going up into the village. Meals are served on the covered terrace on pink table-cloths. The downstairs rooms of the hotel are delightful; the yellow sitting-room has pale-blue chairs.

Nearby Avignon; Aix; the villages of the Luberon.

84480 Bonnieux
Tel 04 90 75 80 78
Fax 04 90 75 96 00
Location on a lower road of the village
Meals all
Prices FF
Rooms 10; 6 double, 4 twin; 9 with bath; all with phone and heating; TV on request
Facilities Garden, terrace
Credit cards MC, EC, V
Children not accepted
Disabled impossible
Pets dogs and cats welcome; 30F a day
Closed beginning of Nov to beginning of March
Director Mme Contaz

Provence-Côte d'Azur

Medieval inn, Haut-de-Cagnes (Alpes-Maritimes)

Le Cagnard

A reader's report raised some doubts about this lovely hotel, perched along the ramparts of an old hill village – specifically about standards of service in the Michelin-starred restaurant. It is far from the most expensive hotel in the Relais & Châteaux group, but it is pricey enough for expectations in this department to be high. Off went an inspector; happily, all was well.

Le Cagnard has been sensitively converted from a series of medieval houses, most with separate street entrances. In the main house there is a stunning medieval vaulted dining-room where you eat by candle-light. But the real knock-out is the upper dining-room, leading out on to the terrace: its elaborate painted ceiling slides away at the touch of a button, opening the room to the sky. The bedrooms vary widely; most retain a medieval feel, thanks to the preservation of features such as stone floors, and are furnished with style, but incongruous exceptions remain. Three rooms in one house have a lovely flowery garden. Access in anything other than a small car is tricky, and getting to some rooms involves a bit of awkward suitcase-lugging.

Nearby Château Grimaldi – modern art museum, with Renaissance courtyard; Nice (15 km); Grasse (30 km) – perfumes.

Rue Pontis-Long
Haut-de-Cagnes
06800 Cagnes-sur-Mer
Tel 04.93.20.73.21
Fax 04.93.22.06.39
Location in middle of hill village, 2 km above main town of Cagnes; car parking 300 m away at entrance to village
Meals breakfast, lunch, dinner
Prices FF-FFFF+
Rooms 18 double, 10 apartments, all with bath; all rooms have central heating, phone, TV, minibar; most have air-conditioning
Facilities dining-room, bar
Credit cards AE, DC, MC, V
Children accepted
Disabled no special facilities
Pets accepted
Closed restaurant only, Thu lunch and Nov to mid-Dec
Proprietors Barel Laroche family

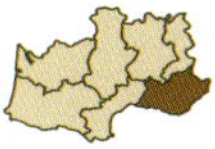

Provence-Côte d'Azur

Town hotel, Cassis (Bouches-du-Rhône)

Le Clos des Arômes

This is a very pretty small hotel, in a quiet street near the old port and run and completely redecorated by the young, friendly and informal Bonnets, who took over from the previous owners four years ago. However, the history of the hotel goes back 50 years and there is a little oil-painting of it as it was in the dining-room. It is bright and sunny, entered either off the street into a large, attractive dining-room or through the paved garden, which is a delight. The dining-room has old terracotta tiles on the floor, stripped wooden panelling on the walls, a big stone fireplace at one end and little tables with blue and yellow cloths and painted blue chairs. Bedrooms are on the two floors above; stairs are steep. Behind simple white-painted doors, rooms are small, but very pretty. Each one has a different colour scheme: fabrics, wallpapers and paintwork are carefully co-ordinated. Furniture is quality country-style reproduction.

Bathrooms are smallish, but spotlessly clean and sparkling white. There are two tiny rooms, with double beds, but usually let as singles. They offer hardly any room to move, but are nonetheless very appealing. The Provençal menu here is very reasonably priced.
Nearby Marseille (20 km); Aix-en-Provence (35 km).

10, rue Paul Mouton
13260 Cassis
Tel 04 42 01 71 84
Fax 04 42 01 31 76
Location in quiet side-street in old town, near port
Meals all
Prices F-FF
Rooms 5 double, 2 single, 1 family; 3 with bath; all with phone and heating
Facilities dining-room; terrace; garden; garage 50F a day
Credit cards all except DC
Children accepted
Disabled not suitable
Pets accepted
Closed beg Oct to end April
Proprietor M Fabrice Bonnet

Provence-Côte d'Azur

Town inn, Château-Arnoux (Alpes-de-Haute-Provence)

La Bonne Étape

'Exceptional food, impeccable service, beautiful pool and rooms – worth every franc,' says a recent customer of this 'good stopover' – a former coaching inn in an unremarkable small town. Outside, it gives little hint of what lies within – one of the most satisfactory blends of refinement and hospitality to be found in France. The kitchen has just lost its second Michelin star; we would like to reaward it. Chefs Pierre and Jany Gleize (father and son) make innovative and stylish use of largely home-grown ingredients. A house speciality is Sisteron lamb (raised on mountain pastures): try it with a deep-red local Vacqueyras Côtes du Rhone. Tables in the formal dining-room have fresh flowers; Bach plays in the background. There are serious eaters here, many alone. The atmosphere is slightly hushed, but the waiters helpful and friendly. There is a charming bar with painted beams. But this is no restaurant-with-rooms. Bedrooms are luxuriously comfortable – beautifully decorated with a tasteful mix of modern and antique pieces. Some have marble bathrooms. The Gleize family are warmly welcoming hosts, happily committed to their work,and have just opened a new restaurant nearby.

Nearby Sisteron – citadel; hill walking.

Chemin du Lac
04160 Château-Arnoux
Tel 04 92 64 00 09
Fax 04 92 64 37 36
Location just off main RN 85 14 km SE of Sisteron (motorway 3km)
Meals all
Prices FFF-FFFF
Rooms 19; 10 doubles, 9 twin, all with bath, shower, phone, sat TV, central heating, air-conditioning, minibar, hairdryer
Facilities heated swimming-pool; terrace; car parking; garage; garden
Credit cards AE,DC,V,EC
Children accepted
Disabled new ground-floor rooms
Pets dogs welcome
Closed 3rd Jan to 12th Feb
Proprietors Gleize family

Provence-Côte d'Azur

Village hotel, Crillon-le-Brave (Vaucluse)

Hostellerie de Crillon le Brave

'Delightful,' enthuses one satisfied visitor to this luxurious hotel occupying the old vicarage in the hilltop village of Crillon-le-Brave. 'Very good restaurant, excellent service, a lovely setting and a charming *patron*.'

The rambling 16thC stone-built house is solid and calm, but most of the credit for the resounding success of the hotel – open only since late 1989 – must go to the aforementioned *patron*, Peter Chittick, a Canadian lawyer with exceptionally clear ideas about hotel-keeping. A considerable share goes also to the perched location, giving uninterrupted views of a heavenly landscape of olive groves and vineyards.

The central trick that Mr Chittick and his collaborator Craig Miller have pulled off is to provide luxury without erasing character. Despite the designer fabrics, fitted carpets and smart bathrooms, the exposed beams, white walls and rustic furniture dominate both in the sitting-rooms and the spacious bedrooms. You eat beneath stone vaults, or out on the pretty terrace. Chef Philippe Monti produces refined Provençal food that is in perfect harmony with this blissful setting.

Nearby Mont Ventoux; Orange (35 km); Avignon; Gordes.

Place de l'Église
84410 Crillon-le-Brave
Tel 04.90.65.61.61
Fax 04.90.65.62.86
Location in hilltop village 35 km NE of Avignon, on D138 off D974, with garden, private car parking and garages
Meals breakfast, lunch (Sat and Sun only), dinner, snacks
Prices FFF-FFFF+
Rooms 19 double (7 twin), 18 with bath, one with shower; 5 suites; all rooms have central heating, phone, minibar, hairdryer
Facilities 3 sitting-rooms, dining-room; swimming-pool
Credit cards AE, MC, V
Children welcome; baby-sitting available
Disabled access difficult
Pets accepted
Closed Jan to Mar
Proprietors Peter Chittick and Craig Miller

Provence-Côte d'Azur

Country hotel, Les Essareaux (Vaucluse)

La Manescale

The King of Belgium has slept here. No doubt, like so many others, he was charmed by all he found in this remote former shepherd's house up in the hills. The thoughtfulness of owners, M and Mme Warland, permeates what could be described as a pocket-sized hotel with every comfort. The smallest details are attended to, here, from towels for the swimming-pool to a small library for serious readers and helpfully labelled light switches. Mme Warland, in her apron, cooks in the kitchen and gathers fresh flowers for the tables before meals; M Warland prints out the menu on his fax machine and delivers her delicious dishes, such as *magret de canard* with apples and bilberries, to diners. Stone steps and pathways connect the main building to garden rooms, each giving privacy and views of the forest and hillsides. Two rooms are named after M Warland's favourite painters – Tiepolo and Dalì. A place for lovers of quiet and of nature, there are numerous paths through the woods for long walks. Classical music plays on the terrace at aperitif time; the views across vineyards and valleys to Mont Ventoux in the distance are superb. It's a steep walk from parking to hotel: a luggage trolley is provided.
Nearby Vaison-la-Romaine (7 km); Côtes du Rhône vineyards.

Route de Faucon
Les Essareaux
84340 Entrechaux
Tel 04 90 46 03 80
Fax 04 90 46 03 89
Location in the hills
Meals breakfast and dinner
Prices FF
Rooms 5; 2 with bath, 3 with shower; all with phone, TV, heating, minibar
Facilities swimming-pool, terrace, gardens, secure parking
Credit cards AE, DC, V, EC, MC
Children welcome if well behaved
Disabled impossible
Pets dogs permitted
Closed end Oct to Easter
Proprietors M and Mme Warland

Provence-Côte d'Azur

Village hotel, Eygalières (Bouches-du-Rhône)

Auberge Provençale

This 18thC former coaching inn has a paved courtyard with trees and potted plants and small marble-topped tables and is well-known locally for its excellent Provençal dishes. 'The chef is not a cook, he's a painter,' said one customer, looking at a little goat's cheese, with fresh green herbs, olive oil and pink peppercorns arranged on the plate before him. The horses' stone drinking troughs remain and guests' cars are safely locked away for the night in the magnificent coachhouse, which has a great arched gateway out into the street.

Owner and chef Didier Pézeril has only recently decided to extend his hospitality to rooms, some of which look out into the courtyard, and they are as deliberately and charmingly evocative of the 19thC as is the bar below. Our inspector's room had blue-washed walls, rough white cotton curtains and a paisley cover on the bed and a view out of the window of the lively Progrès café opposite. Tiled floors are attractively uneven and some rooms have traditional cupboards set in the walls. M Pézeril's philosophy is correspondingly down-to-earth: "We're an *auberge*, we don't have pretensions to be anything else." The whole place oozes character.
Nearby St-Rémy-de-Provence; Les Baux-de-Provence; the Alpilles.

Place de la Mairie
13810 Eygalières
Tel 04 90 95 91 00
Location in the village
Meals all
Prices F-FF
Rooms 5; 4 double, 1 with 2 double beds; 4 with bath, 1 with shower; all with phone and heating; 4 with TV
Facilities courtyard, covered terrace, bar, secure car parking
Credit cards MC, EC, V
Children welcome
Disabled no facilities
Pets well-behaved dogs welcome
Closed beg Nov to mid-Dec
Proprietors Pézeril family

Provence-Côte d'Azur

Converted mill, Fayence (Var)

Moulin de la Camandoule

Our inspector finds changes at this lovingly restored olive mill, with a Roman aqueduct in the extensive grounds. The existing building dates from the 19thC and was rescued some years ago.

Owners Shirley and Wolf Rilla (an English-German couple) moved here in 1986 and business has been increasingly good. The mill now features in glossy magazines and with reason. In summer, meals are served outside on a terrace overlooking a cherry orchard, or by the pool – or in the delightfully rustic dining-room decorated with original mill trappings. The old water wheel is still in the house, preserved behind glass. The atmosphere is very relaxed and the Rillas are charming hosts. Mme Rilla – a former food writer – prepares the light lunches by the pool in the summer herself, but she has a new chef. Menus are short and uncomplicated with the emphasis on Provençal dishes. There's an extra double room – white and apricot – in the tower, satellite TV in all the rooms and new rattan chairs – from India – for the terrace. The beds have recently been replaced, but our inspector noted that rooms are still not all of the same standard. However, the charm is as seductive as ever.

Nearby Grasse (30 km); Cannes (30 km).

Chemin Notre-Dame-des-Cyprès
83440 Fayence
Tel 04 94 76 00 84
Fax 04 94 76 10 40
Location near village in large grounds with car parking
Meals all
Prices FF
(demi-pension and 3 days minimum stay normally obligatory in high season)
Rooms 12; 10 double, 2 single; 8 with bath, 4 with shower; all with phone, heating, sat TV
Facilities pool; gardens; terraces; cherry orchard; dining-room; sitting-room
Credit card MC, V
Children accepted
Disabled not suitable
Pets welcome; 40F a day
Closed never
Proprietors M and Mme Rilla

Provence-Côte d'Azur

Converted mill, Fontvieille (Bouches-du-Rhône)

La Régalido

We continue to be fond of this 19thC oil mill, a Relais & Chateaux place which manages to remain informal and friendly despite its elegant furnishings and high prices – largely thanks to the presence at all hours of the welcoming and helpful Jean-Pierre Michel, chef-proprietor.

The Régalido has been converted into a fine *auberge* in a thoroughly Provençal style, decorated with great flair by Mme Michel. There is a charming sitting-room full of flowers, and a log fire lit on chilly days. Tables are beautifully set in the elegant, peaceful, stone-vaulted dining-room, and there is an atmosphere of well-being which suits the excellent cooking of Jean-Pierre. His style is classic, but he has a penchant for Provençal dishes (seafood, olive oil, herbs and garlic) – and terracotta or cast-iron pots appear alongside the silver salvers.

Bedrooms are individually decorated, and very comfortable, with lots of extras in the well-equipped bathrooms. Friendly staff and a pretty, flowery garden – with a terrace surrounded by mimosa and shaded by fig and olive trees – complete the picture.

Nearby Montmajour Abbey; Arles; the Camargue (10 km) – flamingos, white horses; Tarascon (15 km) – château.

Rue Frédéric-Mistral
13990 Fontvieille
Tel 04.90.54.60.22
Fax 04.90.54.64.29
Location in middle of village, 9 km NE of Arles; with gardens and ample car parking
Meals breakfast, lunch, dinner
Prices FFF-FFFF
Rooms 15 double, 12 with bath, 2 with shower; all rooms have central heating, air-conditioning, phone, minibar
Facilities dining-room, 2 sitting-rooms, bar
Credit cards AE, DC, MC, V
Children accepted
Disabled 1 specially equipped ground-floor bedroom
Pets accepted (at a charge)
Closed Jan; restaurant only, Mon and Tue lunch, Mon dinner in low season
Proprietor Jean-Pierre Michel

Provence-Côte d'Azur

Country hotel, Forcalquier (Alpes-de-Haute-Provence)

Auberge Charembeau

The demand among the French for 'green' holidays, with plenty of fresh air and calm has come at just the right time for André Berger and his English-speaking wife Sandra.

Their 18thC farmhouse, set among fields and trees, has been attractively adapted to retain its original character and provide modern amenities; the old stables have become bedrooms and the attics, where silkworms were bred, are now large, airy suites with a terrace. There is a dry-stone wall around the swimming-pool, which was once the kitchen garden, and the Bergers' free-range hens are much in evidence (they provide eggs for breakfast). But the unusual feature here is a selection of rooms with small holiday kitchens for those who, while in Provence, feel like doing their own cooking after visiting the market. Breakfast is served out on the lawn; at lunchtime there's a *plateau piscine* with wine, served out by the pool. The Bergers have created a charming atmosphere; they are constantly looking to see what more they can do to make their guests even more relaxed and comfortable. In early summer, the *auberge* is surrounded by fields of poppies; the house is well off the road up a long track.

Nearby Forcalquier (3 km); the Montagne de Lure; perched villages.

Route de Niozelles
04300 Forcalquier
Tel 04 92 75 05 69
Fax 04 92 75 24 37
Location on a 7-hectare country estate
Meals breakfast, light lunch
Prices F
Rooms 14; 5 with bath, 9 with shower, 6 with kitchen; all with phone; most with TV
Facilities swimming-pool, tennis court, bicycles
Credit cards V, EC, AE
Children welcome
Disabled no facilities
Pets dogs and cats welcome; 20F a day
Closed Dec and Jan
Proprietors M and Mme Berger

Provence-Côte d'Azur

Village inn, Fox-Amphoux (Var)

Auberge du Vieux Fox

This charming little village, rich in history, has nothing to do with foxes – the name comes from its Roman origins. The inn – in the *place* – was once a priory attached to the 12thC church. Where owner, M Staudinger, now has his reception desk was a sacristy, with a door leading directly into the church, the bells of which ring out every half hour. The Staudingers have been in the international hospitality business for 36 years – and it shows. There is a warm welcome here for visitors; M Staudinger, normally to be found in his beamed reception area with his cat, Fu-fu, is happy to talk about the life and times of Fox-Amphoux and the surrounding area for hours. Bedrooms are carpeted and some newly renovated; curtains and bedspreads are are in fresh, bright colours. Two small rooms in the tower were once monks' cells. Bathrooms are spotlessly clean. (M Staudinger believes there is no excuse for drabness or dirt.) There are comfortable leather armchairs in the *salon* and a piano room, TV and video room, a library and a billiard table. The outside terraces have fine views over Aix and the Alps of Haute Provence. Fish is delivered from Marseille and there's an emphasis on fresh farm produce.

Nearby Lac de Sainte-Croix; Verdon Gorges

Fox-Amphoux
83670 Barjols
Tel 04 94 80 71 69
Fax 04 94 80 78 38
Location in centre of small perched village
Meals all
Prices F
Rooms 8 double; 6 with bath, 2 with shower; all with phone, heating and hairdryer
Facilities sitting- and dining-rooms; terraces, swimming-pool and tennis court 4 km
Credit cards AE, DC, MC, V
Children not encouraged
Disabled no facilities
Pets welcome; 35F per day for large dogs
Closed Never
Proprietors M and Mme Rudolf Staudinger

Provence-Côte d'Azur

Country hotel, Gémenos (Bouches-du-Rhône)

Relais de la Magdeleine

'If only there were more hotels like this,' begins our latest enthusiastic reader's report on this lovely old *bastide*. We share the sentiment: for those of us who can't or won't pay the prices (or don't like the style) of Relais & Châteaux places, a gracious country house like this is quite a find.

It is a family affair. Daniel Marignane's mother opened the hotel in 1932, he and his wife now run the hotel with great charm and good humour, and their son is now in charge of the kitchen – and achieving great things. Improvements are being made all the time; many of the bedrooms have been (charmingly) redecorated. All – even the cheapest ones – in the most elegant country taste, with delightful fabrics (often on the walls, too) and antiques and pictures collected by the Marignanes on their travels. New fixtures and fittings in the bathrooms to the highest of standards.

One of the three dining-rooms has been sandblasted to expose wooden vaultings and beams in a lovely, light wood the colour of honey. It is worth going miles out of one's way to be so warmly welcomed by the family to such a beautiful house. There's a pool – and a donkey – in the garden.

Nearby Cassis (15 km); Marseille (23 km); Aix-en-Provence (25 km).

13420 Gémenos
Tel 04 42 32 20 16
Fax 04 42 32 02 26
Location on edge of town in large grounds, with pool
Meals all
Prices FF
Rooms 24 double; 20 with bath, 4 with shower; 12 twin; all with phone, sat TV, heating
Facilities gardens; pool; sitting-rooms; terrace; lift to 2nd floor; parking
Credit cards MC, V
Children accepted
Disabled lift
Pets accepted
Closed 1st Dec to 15th March
Proprietors M and Mme Marignane

Provence-Côte d'Azur

Village hotel, Grimaud (Var)

Le Coteau Fleuri

The Coteau Fleuri is a delightful and comfortable place to stay, as well as having a superb restaurant – and it is value for money. The old stone house is built on a hillside on the edge of Grimaud village and has a rambling garden with olive trees and a small flowery terrace.

Inside, the atmosphere is rustic, uncluttered, warmly inviting: fine, polished terracotta tiles, white walls and strikingly beautiful, large, simple arrangements of fresh flowers. Bedrooms – some are small – have pretty furnishings and prints. The dining terrace, with wood-panelled roof, Provençal table-cloths, rustic wooden chairs and bougainvillea spilling over the walls, is a delightful place to be in the evening, watching the sun go down over the vineyards. The food is excellent, with plenty of fresh fish and vegetables on the menu and very reasonably priced and well served.

Proprietor M Minard is a relaxed *patron*; his idea of a hotel or restaurant is that it should be an overall positive experience. It's no good having a wonderful meal only to go up to bed in an ugly room, or to sit in an uncomfortable chair to smoke your after-dinner cigar. A hotel must have a soul, he says; his does.

Nearby St-Tropez (10 km); Pampelonne (15 km).

Place des Penitents
83360 Grimaud-Village
Tel 04 94 43 20 17
Fax 04 94 43 33 42
Location on edge of village, with small garden and terrace
Meals all
Prices F-FF
Rooms 13 double; 5 twin; 9 with bath, 5 with shower; all with phone, heating; 1 family room with bath
Facilities dining-room; sitting-room; bar; car parking
Credit cards AE, MC, V
Children welcome
Disabled no facilities
Pets accepted if well behaved
Closed 2 weeks before Xmas and 2 weeks after New Year
Proprietors M and Mme Minard

Provence-Côte d'Azur

Country hotel, Grimaud (Var)

Le Verger

Only a short distance from the massed traffic jams of the Ste-Maxime–St-Tropez road is this haven of peace and green, with wonderful smooth lawns, mature walnut trees, hydrangeas and even a little stream. There's plenty of shade for sitting under and looking up at the dry surrounding hills.

The house is typically Provençal, low, pale pink, white-shuttered, with a shallow tiled roof and on two storeys. French windows from ground-floor bedrooms open directly on to the lawn – and then to the pool. Upstairs rooms have private balconies. Decoration is simple: white walls, Provençal prints, antique, country furniture and big beds. Meals are served outside in summer, on a partly covered terrace – with wisteria – looking out to woods and hills, or, in cooler weather, before an open fire in the large dining-room, which is the only public room.

It is a very unpretentious hotel: relaxed, informal, quiet, and proprietor Anne Zachary is a delightful hostess. Her husband, an experienced chef with quite a local following, cooks interesting, varied dishes and – unusually for the South – likes sauces with cream. A cool, green, quiet oasis.

Nearby St-Tropez (12 km); Provence countryside.

Route de Collobrières
83360 Grimaud
Tel 04 94 43 25 93
Fax 04 94 43 33 92
Location on D14, off D558, in countryside 1 km out of Grimaud, with garden
Meals all
Prices FF
Rooms 8 double; 6 with bath, 2 with shower; all with phone, heating, sat TV; 3 with air-conditioning
Facilities swimming-pool, terrace, garden, parking
Credit cards all except AE
Children not suitable
Disabled 1 room
Pets welcome
Closed Nov to Easter
Proprietor Mme Zachary

Provence-Côte d'Azur

Country hotel, Joucas (Vaucluse)

Le Mas des Herbes Blanches

This is not an authentic *mas,* but a purpose-built hotel; all a bit too perfect to be old, though lizards nip in and out of the dry-stone walls and birds love the TV aerials. Nature is mellowing the hard edges. It is very Relais & Chateaux, with four-star comfort and a Michelin star, flight-attendant-type receptionist at the desk and uninspiring bland fabrics and furniture. It is also increasingly fashionable with those who have been driven inland by the noise and crowds on the coast. Peter Mayle and Mitterrand's 'champagne socialists' have given this part of Provence star status. Many rooms have air-conditioning and balconies, giving sunbathing privacy; there are thick towelling robes for the swimming-pool. Director M Labourie is doing his best to deformalise the place. 'People are on holiday,' he says. 'They don't want three waiters fussing around their table.'

In the evening, though, the view from the hotel to the Grand Luberon becomes almost magical in the gold and pink of the sunset. A chorus of small green frogs accompanies dinner on the terrace and across the valley are the twinkling lights of villages on distant hills: it is an astounding sight.

Nearby Gordes; Apt; Orange; Avignon.

Joucas
84220 Gordes
Tel 04 90 05 79 79
Fax 04 90 05 71 96
Location in countryside above the village of Joucas on the D102
Meals all
Prices FFFF
Rooms 19; all with bath, phone, TV, heating; some with air-conditioning
Facilities pool, secure covered parking, terraces, garden, tennis court
Credit cards AE, DC.
Children welcome
Disabled no facilities
Pets dogs accepted; 60F a day
Closed beg Jan to beg March
Director Jean-Luc Labourie

Provence-Côte d'Azur

Country mas, Mougins (Alpes-Maritimes)

Le Mas Candille

This 18thC farmhouse, near fashionable Mougins, has been a hotel for 30 years – it's a solid building the colour of honey, with wrought-iron balconies and heavy shutters. Inside, the decoration is elegantly rustic, with terracotta flagstones on the floor, simple white walls, low ceilings and heavy oak beams. There are thoughtfully-placed tables, chairs and reading lamps for a quiet moment in the numerous nooks and crannies. The dining-room opens on to a terrace, which has superb views towards Grasse. Our inspector's bedroom – with sloping beamed roof and pretty floral prints – was, unfortunately, next to the boiler-room. Apologies were made for the noise. Artificial flowers in rather large arrangements were also noticed. Outside, there are two pools: a larger heated one and a smaller pool nearby in a quiet and secluded leafy glade. There are all kinds of inducements offered: a free glass of champagne on arrival, free places in the restaurant – the chef is a Roger Vergé trainee – for every party of four.

Our inspector, who found the hotel very comfortable, relaxed and good value, was a little uneasy, though, about uniformed staff sporting name badges.

Nearby Cannes; Grasse; Picasso museum at Vallauris (10 km).

Boulevard Rebuffel
06250 Mougins
Tel 04 93 90 00 85
Fax 04 92 92 85 56
Location in extensive grounds just outside Mougins
Meals all
Prices FFFF
Rooms 21; 20 with bath, 1 with shower; all with twin beds, phone, sat TV, heating, air-conditioning, minibar, hairdryer, safe
Facilities 2 pools; tennis court; parking; 4 international golf courses nearby
Credit cards all
Children accepted
Disabled some ground-floor rooms
Pets accepted
Closed 1st Nov to 31st March
Manager M Galvez

Provence-Côte d'Azur

Village hotel, Mougins (Alpes-Maritimes)

Les Muscadins

This cluster of houses – set in a small tropical garden with spectacular views down to the coast at Cannes – has been an hotel for many years. (Picasso is said to have stayed here as a young man and tried, unsuccessfully, to pay his bill by painting murals on the walls of his room.) Now painted gleaming white and luxuriously comfortable, it has been run since 1992 by charming, amusing American owner, Eddie Bianchini, who is passionate about golfing (sporting prints abound) and food.

Bouncing back from the loss of the house's Michelin star a few years ago, he has radically changed the food concept with menus based on creatively prepared fresh produce, and kept prices down, earning him acclaim from Gault-Millau. He's also imbued the place with a friendly, relaxed atmosphere and his own personal interests and taste. Many of his collection of antiques once belonged to 18thC fops known as *Muscadins*. Bedrooms – all with marble bathrooms and some with sea views – are beautifully furnished and decorated, with white walls and co-ordinated fabrics. (A hideous new garage has spoiled views from rooms at the rear, much to M Bianchini's wrath.) Elegant terrace.

Nearby Cannes; Grasse; Picasso museum at Vallauris (10 km).

18 Boulevard Courteline
06250 Mougins
Tel 04 93 90 00 43
Fax 04 92 92 88 23
Location on E road into old village, 2 km from A8 motorway, 6 km N of Cannes, with parking
Meals all
Prices FFF-FFFF
Rooms 8 and 1 suite; all with bath, phone, sat TV, heating, air-conditioning, hairdryer, safe
Facilities bar; sitting-room; dining-room; veranda; terrace
Credit cards all
Children welcome
Disabled no special facilities
Pets welcome
Closed 12th to 20th Dec; 15th Feb to 15th Mar
Proprietor M Bianchini

Provence-Côte d'Azur

Country house hotel, Moustiers-Ste.-Marie (Alpes de H.-P.)

La Bastide de Moustiers

This is the *madeleine* of chef Alain Ducasse, who has three Michelin stars for his cooking at the Hotel de Paris in Monte Carlo. In a pale pink restored 17thC *bastide* overlooking green meadows on the edge of a village near the dramatic Verdon gorge, he has created his own remembrance of times past. His country house for lovers of Provence is a resounding triumph; delicious smells of cooking come from the kitchen all day. Chefs, in their whites, can be seen collecting salad and fresh herbs from a vegetable garden which is a work of art in itself.The *bastide* and the discreet swimming-pool are surrounded by beds of lavender and each of the seven romantically decorated bedrooms evokes a colour or an image of Provence. There is not enough room here properly to praise M Ducasse's creation, or the welcome provided by his enthusiastic young staff. To sit on M Ducasse's terrace in the morning air with a bowl of *café au lait*, fresh bread from the village bakery and home-made rhubarb jam among green glazed pots overflowing with white petunias is a moment to be treasured. Dinner is just as memorable; traditional dishes with plenty of olive oil and garden vegetables. Upstairs, the sheets are being turned down as you eat.
Nearby Moustiers ceramics; Lake Sainte-Croix; gorges.

La Grisolière
04360 Moustiers-Ste-Marie
Tel 04 92 70 47 47
Fax 04 92 70 47 48
Location within walking distance of Moustiers
Meals all
Prices FFF-FFFF
Rooms 7 double; all with bath, shower, phone,TV, heating, air-conditioning, minibar, hairdryer
Facilities pool, riding, bicycles, parking
Credit cards AE, MC, V
Children welcome
Disabled 1 accessible room
Pets no
Closed 1st Feb to 15th March
Proprietor A Ducasse

Provence-Côte d'Azur

Village inn, Peillon-Village (Alpes-Maritimes)

Auberge de la Madone

A recent visitor described the setting of this hotel as 'stunning'. 'Delightful' was the one-word verdict offered by another reader on this top-of-the-range Logis, which happily combines a sense of special hospitality with affordable (though not low) prices. The Millos have just opened an annexe in the old part of the village – the Auberge du Pourtail. Rooms here are less expensive and you take your meals at the Madone.

You may think that you have taken a wrong turning as you first spy Peillon, perched impossibly above, with little sign of any road leading up. Time stands still here. The medieval village consists of a few dark cobbled alleys leading up to the church, and tall stone houses looking out over rocky crests and distant forests.

The *auberge* is set just outside the walled village. Behind, paths lead off into the hills, past the grazing sheep with their tinkling bells; in front is the village car park and *boules* area. Within, the rather small bedrooms (with equally small balconies) are attractive and comfortable with stylish all-white bathrooms. Meals are served on the pretty, sunny terrace, under a large awning, or in the welcoming Provençal-style dining-room. Cooking is above average.
Nearby Monaco – Palace, museums, exotic gardens.

06440 Peillon-Village
Tel 04.93.79.91.17
Fax 04.93.79.99.36
Location on edge of perched village, 19 km NE of Nice; with ample car parking
Meals breakfast, lunch, dinner
Prices FF-FFF
Rooms 20 double, 15 with bath, 5 with shower; all rooms have central heating, phone, TV
Facilities bar, 2 dining-rooms; tennis court
Credit cards MC, V
Children very welcome
Disabled no special facilities
Pets accepted by arrangement
Closed mid-Oct to mid-Dec, 2 weeks Jan
Proprietors Millo family

Provence-Côte d'Azur

Auberge de l'Orangerie

This curious little *auberge,* almost submerged by a jungle of greenery, is just off the main street of a small town that prides itself on its garlic festival. Owners Gerard and Micky Delarocque have given an original and imaginative 'retro' feeling to an 18thC house in a gated courtyard. Downstairs is the lively restaurant, which draws in local business people at lunchtime with dishes like *filets de rascasse à la provençale* and *noisettes de gigot d'agneau au basilic frais.* In the dining-room are striking pictures by Georges de La Tour, which are, in fact, painted by M Delarocque, a talented copyist (and single-malt connoisseur).

But the real fun starts upstairs, with Mme's clever, evocative décor and her charming written 'thoughts' on the theme of each room, which hang framed on the walls. The George Sand room has a portrait of the writer by Delacroix – or could it be a copy by M Delarocque? The room named after Mme Récamier has in it a *chaise-longue* like the ones she made so fashionable. Behind the Bohemianism, though, is a professional management, with orthodox ideas on things such as rules: no washing of clothes in bedrooms, for example.

Nearby Orange (5 km).

4, rue de l'Ormeau
84420 Piolenc
Tel 04 90 29 59 88
Fax 04 90 29 67 74
Location in side-street
Meals all
Prices F
Rooms 5; 2 with bath, 3 with shower; all with TV and heating
Facilities terrace; garden; secure parking
Credit cards V, EC, MC
Children accepted
Disabled no facilities
Pets dogs accepted; 40F a day
Closed never
Proprietors M and Mme Delarocque

Provence-Côte d'Azur

Suburban hotel, Le Pontet-Avignon (Vaucluse)

Auberge de Cassagne

Le Pontet, a suburb of Avignon with wide, busy roads and new housing developments, does not appear to be a place where anyone might find a hotel of any interest, let alone charm. However, behind a high wall is a former cottage of the nearby *château* which has been turned, with much hard work, into a remarkably comfortable and pleasant hotel, with a locally renowned one-Michelin-star kitchen, chef from Bocuse, and an abundant wine cellar. At dinner, our inspector counted 20 different cheeses on the tray and 45 Côtes du Rhône reds on the wine list. In somewhat confined grounds, the hotel also manages, with resourceful use of lawns, paths and landscaped gardens, to create an impression of space and even rusticity. Everything is immaculately well-tended; the cypress trees look as if someone brushes and combs them every night. Bedrooms in the garden bungalows are large and pretty, with fresh, Provençal prints; each one has its own terrace, with table and chairs, where guests can have breakfast in dressing-gowns – and do. Rooms 16 and 17 are almost in the swimming-pool and delightfully secluded and quiet in the evenings, when the restaurant – a popular gathering place – is buzzing with local clientele.
Nearby Avignon; Aix-en-Provence (82 km); Arles (36 km).

450 Allée de Cassagne
84130 Le Pontet-Avignon
Tel 04 90 31 04 18
Fax 04 90 32 25 09
Location in a quiet suburban side-road
Meals all
Prices FFF
Rooms 30 double; 28 with bath, 2 with shower; all with phone, sat TV, air-conditioning, heating, minibar, hairdryer, safe
Facilities pool; garden; tennis court; boules; 18-hole golf course 3 km; secure parking
Credit cards AE, DC, MC, V, EC
Children welcome; baby-sitting service available
Disabled 3 rooms equipped for handicapped
Pets accepted; 60F a day
Closed never
Proprietors M Gallon, M Trestour, M Boucher

Provence-Côte d'Azur

Island hotel, Porquerolles (Var)

Auberge des Glycines

There are no cars on the island of Porquerolles and when the day-trippers leave in the evening, peace prevails. This delightful small hotel is a fun, casual, bright and sunny place in the little port of Porquerolles, but within an easy walk are rocky creeks for swimming and splendid diving spots.

Pale yellow with blue shutters, the hotel is built around an inner courtyard, which has lemon trees, wisteria and a fig tree; meals are served here on red Provençal table-cloths under white umbrellas. The entire hotel is decorated with bright, fresh colours and has a charming look of stylish simplicity. Downstairs, there are dried flowers and straw hats on the walls and terracotta tiles on the floor. Bedrooms are variations on a theme: clean, modern bathrooms have pale tiles and white fittings; bedrooms have matching Provençal print bedspreads and curtains. Rooms have little balconies or terraces looking into the courtyard or out towards pine and eucalyptus trees. Food is excellent value: plenty of fresh fish. Our inspector had *loup de mer* flambéed at the table with fennel and grilled in a salt crust that was cracked open before being served. Young, friendly staff.

Nearby beaches; diving; cycling and walking; national park.

Place d'Armes
83400 Porquerolles
Tel 04 94 58 30 36
Fax 04 94 58 35 22
Location in Porquerolles village, 5 minutes from beach; access 20 mins by ferry from La Tour Fondue (Hyères) or water taxi
Meals all
Prices FF
Rooms 12 double, 1 triple; 10 with bath, 3 with shower; all with phone, TV, heating, air-conditioning
Facilities terrace, courtyard, dining-room
Credit cards all except AE
Children welcome
Disabled no facilities
Pets small ones accepted
Closed mid to end Jan
Proprietor Florence Venture

Provence-Côte d'Azur

Country hotel, Ramatuelle (Var)

La Ferme d'Hermès

Mme Verrier has named her charming little hotel after her much-loved late Welsh terrier – there is now a junior version in his place. Our inspector's report is positively glowing: 'This is a gorgeous spot – exquisite.'

The hotel is a recently-built *mas*, now softened by the weather and creepers and surrounded by a mass of trees, shrubs, plants and greenery. Vines come up to the pool. Inside, loving attention is given to detail. Rooms are all white, with terracotta tiles on the floor – burnished with beeswax – and co-ordinated Provençal fabrics. Furniture is old, stripped pine. Each bedroom has its own private terrace and little tiled kitchenette, with gas and electric rings, oven, sink and refrigerator. Tea towels are provided and changed every day. Mme returns from the market every Saturday morning with armfuls of fresh flowers. Breakfast is the only meal served – on each private terrace – and Mme makes her own jam. She thinks of everything for her guests, whom she treats as if they were part of her circle of friends: alarm clock, electrical mosquito repellent, daily room service, iron and ironing board, hairdryer, and even toothbrush (in case it was left at home).

Nearby Ramatuelle (2 km); St-Tropez (10 km); Pampelonne (2 km).

Val de Pons-Rte de l'Escalet
83350 Ramatuelle
Tel 04 94 79 27 80
Fax 04 94 79 26 86
Location in garden down a little lane 2 km from beaches
Meals breakfast
Prices FF-FFF
Rooms 10 double; all with bath, shower, phone, TV, heating, kitchenette
Facilities pool; garden
Credit cards all except AE
Children not encouraged
Disabled no facilities
Pets accepted; 50F a day
Closed 1st Nov to 1st April
Proprietor Mme Verrier

Provence-Côte d'Azur

Country house hotel, Reillanne (Alpes-de-Haute-Provence)

Auberge de Reillanne

'Bizarre, but delightful' is one view of this proudly unconventional hotel, which once had two stars. Proprietor Maurice Bellaiche has not suffered with their loss. Some reports we have had verge on the ecstatic and it's not difficult to see why. Bedrooms in this splendid old house, with stone walls and beamed ceilings, are vast, somewhat plain and functional. What is winning, though, is M Bellaiche's approach to hospitality, which helps to give this place a most individual and relaxed ambience. Striped deckchairs are attractively arranged around the large garden, shaded by tall trees, filled with birds. There are no TVs anywhere, but plenty of books. M Bellaiche, who lives in the unspoiled village nearby, appears in the evening to cook his own uncomplicated dishes; guests otherwise are looked after by his charming assistant. In each bathroom is a basket containing some personal items which M Bellaiche feels might be useful. He hopes he has provided a calm and restful retreat from the turbulence of everyday life. He has. Visitors will never find the hotel full – a full house, in M Bellaiche's opinion, might create undesirable tensions. There are excellent walks in the vicinity.
Nearby Reillanne; Manosque; Apt; Forcalquier.

04110 Reillanne
Tel 04 92 76 45 95
Fax none
Location in countryside, 1 km from village; 19 km SW of Forcalquier
Meals Breakfast and dinner
Prices F
Rooms 7; all with bath, phone, heating, minibar and hairdryer
Facilities parking, large garden
Credit cards EC,V,MC
Children welcome
Disabled not easy
Pets accepted: 50F a day
Closed never
Proprietor M Bellaiche

Provence-Côte d'Azur

Country villa, Roussillon (Vaucluse)

Mas de Garrigon

'We arrived without reservation and were willingly accommodated; the Provençal-style room was very comfortable, the bathroom large and well stocked; the pool was heavenly after a long drive, and the surrounding area pleasant for strolling; dinner was wonderful, with a wide selection and large portions.' A reader reports this is an ideal end to a day's touring.

The ochre-coloured building was purpose-built by the Rech-Druarts in the late 1970s, though you might not guess it: the traditional Provençal farmhouse style has been carefully reproduced, with a multiplicity of rough-tiled roofs facing this way and that, as if built at random over the years. The hotel stands isolated among pines and scrub, facing the Luberon hills. In front of the house is a neat sheltered pool sharing country views with the sunny private terraces of the bedrooms, well-equipped, modern. The place is run on house-party rather than conventional hotel lines. Guests are encouraged to browse in the well-stocked library or listen to classical music in the comfortable *salon* – before an open fire in winter. A new chef, Sylvain Bourlet, has taken over the cooking, but Mme Rech-Druart continues to be much involved in the menu-planning.
Nearby Gordes (7 km) – château; Village des Bories (5 km).

Rte de St-Saturnin d'Apt
Roussillon 84220 Gordes
Tel 04.90.05.63.22
Fax 04.90.05.70.01
Location in countryside, on D2 3 km N of Roussillon, 7 km E of Gordes; in grounds with ample car parking
Meals all
Prices FF-FFF
Rooms 7 double (2 twin), two family rooms, all with bath; all rooms have phone, TV, minibar, terrace
Facilities 3 dining-rooms, bar, library, sitting-room; swimming-pool
Credit cards AE, DC, V
Children older ones accepted if well behaved **Disabled** ground-floor bedrooms
Pets accepted by arrangement
Closed restaurant only, Mon; mid-Nov to Mar
Manager Mme Christiane Rech-Druart

Provence-Côte d'Azur

Country hotel, Les Stes-Maries-de-la-Mer (Bouches-du-Rhône)

Hostellerie du Mas de Cacharel

Half a mile from the road and on a 70-hectare estate adjoining a nature reserve, this small hotel was built in the '60s by film director and photographer Denys Colomb de Daunant, who made the beautiful slow-motion film, *The Dream of the Wild Horses.* Now run by his son, Florian, a former shipbroker, it has remained very simple and unpretentious. There's no TV (much frowned on) and the ground-floor rooms – looking into a courtyard and out to the marshes – are basic, and charming, with white walls and some contain huge grainy photographs of horses. There are also plenty of horses to ride; the family has about 60. With no restaurant, there's a bar and tables in a huge beamed barn, decorated with mounted bulls' horns, cattle bells and farm implements. The centrepiece is a massive 18thC stone fireplace. An *assiette campagnarde* – of ham, goats' cheese and sausages – is served, with wine, from noon to 8 pm. The stables are close by, and can be visited any time. The bird life, all around, is a wonder; there's a constant parade of flamingos. The frenetic tourist activity in Les Stes-Marie-de-la-Mer, 5 km down the road, is in another world. The Colomb de Daunants are delightful hosts.
Nearby Arles (30 km); Aigues-Mortes; Avignon.

Route de Cacharel
13460 Les Stes-Maries-de-la-Mer
Tel 04 90 97 95 44
Fax 04 90 97 87 97
Location in the marshes of the Camargue
Meals breakfast; *assiette compagnarde* with wine 85F
Prices FF
Rooms 11; 8 with bath, 3 with shower; all with phone and heating
Facilities swimming-pool, horses, secure car parking
Credit cards EC, MC, V
Children welcome
Disabled 1 room with wide door
Pets well-behaved dogs accepted
Closed never
Proprietors Colomb de Daunant family

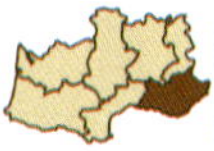

Provence-Côte d'Azur

Country hotel, Les Stes-Maries-de-la-Mer (Bouches-du-Rhône)

Mas de la Fouque

Over a candle-lit dinner, a young woman was confiding to her companion how much she loved him. But his eyes were elsewhere: a large grey heron was wading through the pond. The evening floorshow, as seen through the picture windows here, is extraordinary: white horses and the little black bulls of the Camargue wander through the reeds and grasses of the marshes and squadrons of pink flamingos fly overhead. This Spanish-style whitewashed hotel, on the water's edge, resembles a kind of Southfork; there are saddles in the hall and the attentive and friendly owner M Cochat wears cowboy boots. This, however, is a four-star luxury ranch with a helicopter pad, exotic bathrooms, whirlpool baths and where they like you to dress for dinner. Many of the smartly-decorated rooms – well protected against mosquitoes and with fans – have private terraces built over the lagoon for sunbathing and bird-watching. (Take binoculars.) Plenty of white wicker chairs give a light and airy feel to the *salon*. There's a comfortable bar decorated with illustrations from a turn-of-the century harness catalogue. Food is excellent, with elegantly presented regional dishes; many vegetables and herbs are home grown.

Nearby Les Stes-Maries-de-la-Mer; Aigues-Mortes; Arles.

Route du Petit-Rhône
13460 Les Stes-Marie-de-la-Mer
Tel 04 90 97 81 02
Fax 04 90 97 96 84
Location well off the road on a 4-hectare estate
Meals all
Prices FFFF
Rooms 13; all with bath, phone, TV, heating, air-conditioning, minibar, hairdryer; 4 with whirlpool baths
Facilities swimming-pool, terraces, bicycles, fishing, putting, secure car parking
Credit cards AE, DC, MC, V
Children welcome if well behaved
Disabled 1 room
Pets dogs accepted; 60-80F a day, with meal
Closed 2nd Nov to 25th March
Proprietor M Cochat

Provence-Côte d'Azur

Country villa, St-Paul-de-Vence (Alpes-Maritimes)

Le Hameau

It's a standard pattern among readers reporting on Le Hameau that they stay longer than they planned to, which is about as clear a recommendation as you can get. Not only is it a captivating place, but also it offers very good value. St-Paul-de-Vence is a perfectly preserved hill village. Its ramparts, rising above green terraces of vineyards and bougainvillea, provide panoramic views of the Alpes-Maritimes, and its old streets are lined by galleries, workshops and chic boutiques. Of the few hotels in and around the village, Le Hameau is certainly one of the most desirable – an unusually stylish and notably relaxed place run by a friendly and eager-to-please young couple. It consists of a cluster of red-roofed Provençal villas, surrounded by orange, lemon and other fruit trees. Bedrooms are rustic in style, with beams, dark-wood furniture and rugs on red-tiled floors; they vary considerably in size and price – many have their own terrace or balcony. There is a cool, neat breakfast room, but you will be hoping to have no need of it – one of Le Hameau's great delights is breakfast (with home-made jam) taken in the large terraced garden, which accommodates a small but smart pool.
Nearby Maeght Foundation – contemporary arts; Cagnes-sur-Mer (5 km); Nice (15 km); Grasse (25 km) – perfumes.

528 Route de la Colle
06570 St-Paul-de-Vence
Tel 04.93.32.80.24
Fax 04.93.32.55.75
Location 1 km outside village, 20 km from Nice; with gardens and car parking
Meals breakfast
Prices FF
Rooms 11 double (5 twin), 1 single, 3 suites; all with bath or shower; one children's room ; all rooms have central heating, air-conditioning, phone, minibar, safe
Facilities sitting-room, dining-room; swimming-pool
Credit cards AE, MC, V
Children accepted if well behaved
Disabled no special facilities
Pets accepted if well behaved
Closed mid-Nov to 24 Dec, mid-Jan to mid-Feb
Manager Xavier Huvelin

Provence-Côte d'Azur

Town hotel, St-Rémy-de-Provence (Bouches-du-Rhône)

Mas de Carassins

Mme Ripert's family's farmhouse became a hotel after the '70s drought and she and her husband are disarmingly considerate and courteous hosts. In a quiet, almost rural, part of St-Rémy, with Van Gogh olive groves and close to the Alpilles, it has a large courtyard and extensive, secluded lawned gardens. M Ripert has collected a fund of cultural information about the area in a small sitting-room and provides daily newspapers in the languages of all his guests. Carassin, as he will explain, is the scientific name for goldfish; the goldfish theme runs through the hotel. Room keys are attached to stuffed fabric goldfish; you may have a goldfish mat in your room. There are charming old-fashioned touches. Mme puts a jug of fresh water and garden flowers in all rooms. There's a useful drying-room for washing – and ironing boards. Décor is old-fashioned, too. During the day, M Ripert closes shutters to keep out the heat. Guests are asked to refrain from wearing revealing sunbathing dress near the house – it is permitted in the garden. In the evenings the couple provide "little snacks", such as salad and cheese.

The Roman remains at Glanum are a few minutes' walk away: you can get there before the coaches arrive in the morning.
Nearby Les Baux-de-Provence (7 km); Avignon (20 km).

1 Chemin Gaulois
13210 St-Rémy-de-Provence
Tel 04 90 92 15 48
Fax 04 90 92 63 47
Location in quiet, residential lane
Meals breakfast; evening snacks
Prices FF
Rooms 10; all with double bed, bath, phone, heating
Facilities garden, terrace, secure car parking
Credit cards MC, V, EC
Children accepted
Disabled 1 ground-floor room
Pets not accepted
Closed beg Nov to end March
Proprietors M and Mme Ripert

Provence-Côte d'Azur

Château hotel, St-Rémy-de-Provence (Bouches-du-Rhône)

Château de Roussan

This wonderfully romantic early 18thC château, built by the Marquis de Ganges, a grandson of Nostradamus, arouses strong feelings. "People love it or hate it," says Catherine McHugo, now in charge of management. An avenue of 100-year-old plane trees leads up to the lovely house, which should, one feels, be treated with enormous respect – and it is. There is very little commercialization of the exterior of this grand old place, apart from a few sun umbrellas in the courtyard at the rear. But some bits of it are pretty shabby, so be warned. This is not a modern hotel; a great deal of it is still back in the 18thC. That is its charm. The gracious rooms are beautifully furnished with antiques; on the staircase is a portrait of the Marquise de Ganges. There is a formal library/*salon* in the oldest part of the house and a vaulted breakfast room. The menu for the evening is exhibited on a music stand in the hall and the cuisine is appropriately traditional, with butter and cream. The garden is dreamy; there's a bamboo grove, palm trees, weeping willow and a domed glasshouse for exotic plants. Leading out of the park is a leafy back lane to St-Rémy, a 20-minute walk away.
Nearby Tarascon (15 km); Avignon (30 km); Arles (30 km); the Camargue.

Route de Tarascon
13210 St-Rémy-de-Provence
Tel 04 90 92 11 63
Fax 04 90 92 50 59
Location on the outskirts of St-Rémy; in a large park
Meals all
Prices FF-FFF
Rooms 21; 14 double, 7 twin; 14 with bath, 7 with shower; all with phone, heating
Facilities gardens, terraces, secure car parking, TV room
Credit cards AE, MC, V
Children accepted
Disabled 1 ground-floor room
Pets accepted
Manager Catherine McHugo

Provence-Côte d'Azur

La Ponche

You might not think St-Tropez would be our kind of town, but La Ponche is our kind of hotel, at least when we're feeling like a treat. Tucked away in a tiny square overlooking the small fishing port and tiny beach of La Ponche (where Vadim's *And God Created Woman* was filmed, starring Brigitte Bardot), this cluster of 17thC houses offers a compelling combination of sophistication and warmth. Marguerite Barbier started her fishermen's bar in 1937; later her daughter, Simone Duckstein, steadily transformed it into a stylish, arty four-star hotel, full of personal touches. Paintings by Mme Duckstein's first husband cover the walls.

You can eat on a terrace, looking across a square to the sea, or in one of several areas indoors, including the main dining-room – unpretentious but sophisticated. The food is memorable, particularly the seafood. Bedrooms are captivating and very comfortable. Many have recently been smartly revamped, with stylish colour schemes and slick bathrooms. A couple of noisier bedrooms facing the street may induce you to sleep with the double-glazed windows closed and the air-conditioning on.

Nearby Beaches: Les Graniers (100 m); La Bouillabaisse (1 km); Tahiti (4 km).

3 Rue des Remparts
83990 St-Tropez
Tel 04.94.97.02.53
Fax 04.94.97.78.61
Location in heart of old town, overlooking Port des Pêcheurs; with private garage and valet parking
Meals breakfast, lunch, dinner
Prices FFF-FFFF
Rooms 11 double with bath; 2 family rooms with bath; 2 apartments; 3 suites; all have air-conditioning, central heating, phone, satellite TV, minibar, safe
Facilities TV room, bar, 2 dining-rooms
Credit cards AE, MC, V
Children accepted
Disabled access difficult
Pets accepted
Closed end Oct to end Mar
Proprietor Mme Barbier

Provence-Côte d'Azur

Country hotel, Le Sambuc (Bouches-du-Rhône)

Mas de Peint

This is Camargue *chic,* achieved at lavish expense by the owners, the Bons, whose cattle-branding mark appears on the crisp, white linen in an exquisite little hotel created out of an 18thC stable attached to their own house. Mme Bon, an architect and interior designer, has considerably altered the building to make lovely, spacious rooms with wooden beamed ceilings, sandstone floors, paintwork the colour of sugared almonds and enviable antiques. The whole ensemble feels like a wing for private guests rather than a hotel, which is the way it's meant to be. Everyone eats together at separate tables – sometimes a little awkwardly – in the old-fashioned kitchen, which emanates inviting smells before dinner; vegetables and herbs come from the garden. A harness hangs in the hall, shelves are filled with books, there's a quiet little reading room, and a newspaper for the breakfast table. Jacques Bon, who breeds bulls and horses, is often in and out, inviting visitors to come and see his stock and his farm, on which he grows rice. The bedrooms are in classic country-house style; some have cast-iron baths and little wooden staircases up to a galleried bathroom. There's a discreet swimming-pool hidden from the house.
Nearby Arles; Avignon (36 km); Nîmes (31 km); Aux (76 km).

Le Sambuc
13200 Arles
Tel 04 90 97 20 62
Fax 04 90 97 22 20
Location in open countryside
Meals all
Prices FFFF
Rooms 8 rooms and 2 suites; all with bath, phone, sat TV, heating, air-conditioning, minibar, safe
Facilities swimming-pool, sitting-rooms, covered secure parking, riding, bicycles
Credit cards all
Children welcome; half-price meals for under-10s
Disabled 1 room
Pets dogs accepted; 75F a day
Closed 10th Jan to beg March
Proprietors M and Mme Bon

Provence-Côte d'Azur

Village hotel, Seillans (Var)

Hôtel des Deux Rocs

This captivating blue-shuttered hotel in a charming protected medieval hill village has long been one of our favourites. Nothing changes at the Deux Rocs, which is one of the secrets of its enduring appeal. It conforms to what everyone *expects* of a small unspoiled hotel in Provence, from the pleasures of breakfast by the fountain in the little cobbled square in front, to the brilliant, restrained style of director Mme Hirsch, whose touch is evident everywhere. 'Came for one night, stayed for six,' says a typical entry in the visitors' book. Did that guest, like so many others, fall in love with the wide 18thC staircase, or the bedroom so dashingly decorated in red-and-white checks, or the room with *toile de Jouy* on the walls, or the little downstairs *salon* with the open fireplace and the gigantic TV (none in the rooms here, of course)? Mme Hirsch and her assistant Mme Francine came to Seillans years ago when it was an artists' colony – Max Ernst lived here at the end of his life – and together they give the hotel its gentle civilized air which is so alluring. Bathrooms are old-fashioned, towels are thick, the food traditional and excellent. Parking, though, requires patience.
Nearby Lac de Saint Cassien (15 km); Grasse (32 km); St-Raphaël (33 km); Cannes (47 km); Gorges du Verdon (40 km).

Place Font d'Amont
83440 Seillans
Tel 04 94 76 87 32
Fax 04 94 76 88 68
Location at top of small village
Meals all
Prices F-FF
Rooms 14; 6 with bath, 8 with shower, all with phone and heating
Facilities terrace, bar, sitting-room, dining-room
Credit cards MC, EC, V
Children accepted
Disabled no facilities
Pets accepted, but not in restaurant
Closed 1st Nov to 1st April
Director Mme Hirsch

Provence-Côte d'Azur

Country hotel, Tourtour (Var)

Auberge Saint Pierre

A third generation of Marcellins is now running this hotel which, on a 70-hectare agricultural estate, is surrounded by lush green fields and has its own farm. (The approach, though, through a development of holiday villas gives a worrying first impression.) Little of the old 16thC house can be recognized, but adaptations have been done sympathetically; the TV room was once a chapel. It is the setting which gives this place its charm. There is nothing to be seen for miles except meadows and woods, and a deep calm prevails. Eight of the newer bedrooms have terraces and furniture made from estate-grown oak and elm. Furnishings are plain but attractive; the style is modest yet comfortable. M Marcellin, a disciple of Escoffier, is the chef, and his cuisine uses a wide variety of produce from the family farm, which can be visited by guests and is a short walk away. One of the specialities of the house is a *jambon cru d'agneau fumé.* With swimming-pool, long walks, archery, tennis courts, and fishing in the lake, the Saint Pierre provides everything needed for a complete retreat; it is also a useful base for visiting Tourtour – described as one of the most beautiful villages in France – with its sensational views.
Nearby Tourtour; Lac de Sainte Croix; Verdon Gorges.

Tourtour
83690 Salernes
Tel 04 94 70 57 17
Fax 04 94 70 59 04
Location in countryside
Meals all
Prices FF
Rooms 16; 6 double, 7 twin, 3 with double and single bed; all with phone
Facilities swimming-pool, terraces, tennis court, cycling, archery, fishing, parking
Credit cards CB, MC, V
Children accepted
Disabled no facilities
Pets accepted
Closed 1st October to 3rd March
Proprietors M and Mme Marcellin

Provence-Côte d'Azur

Converted castle, Trigance (Var)

Château de Trigance

For more than 20 years, Jean-Claude Thomas and his wife have run this characterful and comfortable hotel near the dramatic Gorges du Verdon, and they show no signs of flagging. Trigance remains a welcoming port of call in a region of rough terrain and few villages. On arrival, you might be taken aback. Is this fortress, perched high on a rocky peak, really your hotel? (Yes). And if it is, how are you to penetrate its defences? (By climbing a steep flight of 100 steps – don't worry, your bags will be carried up.) Once inside, you are in the Middle Ages. M Thomas has painstakingly rebuilt his 11thC castle stone by stone (villagers stole many of them to build their own houses); he will be delighted to show you photographs of the various stages of his amazing endeavour. The impressive stone-vaulted, candle-lit dining-room (with a knight in armour at the entrance), and the sitting-room below, are windowless and highly atmospheric, furnished in medieval style. Most of the bedrooms (cut into the hill) are similar, with canopied beds, antique furniture, tapestries and banners – and stunning views from their windows. You can have breakfast on the battlements. The cooking is surprisingly good, considering how remote the location is.
Nearby Gorges du Verdon (10 km); Castellane (20 km).

83840 Trigance
Tel 04 94 76 91 18
Fax 04 94 85 68 99
Location at 750 metres, overlooking tiny village, 10 km NW of Comps-sur-Artuby; with terrace and private car parking
Meals all
Prices FF-FFF
Rooms 10 double; all with bath, phone, TV, heating, hairdryer
Facilities dining-room, sitting-room, terraces, tennis court in village; helipad
Credit cards AE, DC, MC, V
Children accepted
Disabled no access
Pets accepted
Closed Nov to mid-March
Proprietors M and Mme Thomas

Provence-Côte d'Azur

Town hotel, Vaison-la-Romaine (Vaucluse)

Hostellerie Le Beffroi

The hotel is composed of two beautiful houses in the same street of this medieval hilltop town – one was built in the 16thC for the Comte de Saint Véran, the other, built in the 17thC, was the home of the Marquis de Taulignan. There are plenty of beams, old stone, and polished red-tiled floors in both and views from the terraces look down to the new town below, which is built around two sites of Roman excavations. (Some of the houses in the old town were built of stone from the ruins.) The Beffroi is above it all – even in the hottest weather there's a fresh breeze.

The friendly, young, and often very busy, proprietor, Yann Christiansen (the hotel has been in the family for three generations now) and his wife, Christine, constantly strive to come up with ways of making the hotel even more comfortable and convenient for their guests. Serving lunchtime salads on the terrace has proved a great success. The cuisine is traditional Provençal; the chef has given demonstrations in California. There are still, however, relatively few rooms with baths. A swimming-pool with fine views of the rooftops below and an ingenious mini-golf course are added attractions.

Nearby Orange (25 km); Avignon (40 km).

Rue de l'Évêché Haute Ville
84110 Vaison-la-Romaine
Tel 04 90 36 04 71
Fax 04 90 36 24 78
Location in the old town, up a steep hill
Meals all
Prices FF
Rooms 22; 8 double, 13 twin, 1 single; 8 with bath, 14 with shower; all with phone, heating, sat TV and minibar
Facilities terraces, garden, pool, mini-golf, 8 car parking places
Credit cards AE, D, V, MC, EC
Children welcome
Disabled not possible
Pets accepted; 35F a day
Closed 15th Feb to 20th March and 11th Nov to 20th Dec
Proprietors M and Mme Christiansen

Provence-Côte d'Azur

Town villa, Vence (Alpes Maritimes)

La Roseraie

The whole feeling of this pale pink *belle époque* villa is of a rambling family house – straw hats and little bunches of dried flowers hang on the walls and there are old photographs and prints. The Ganiers are a charming, helpful and informal young couple, determined to enjoy their work by making sure guests are happy. The mature garden is full of exotic plants and trees – a banana palm, a 100-year-old giant magnolia, orange trees and oleander. The reception area/sitting-room is immediately inviting, with low beamed ceiling, little stone fireplace, Provençal fabrics, and pleasing objects like old travelling trunks and an antique rocking horse. Our inspector noted that Bach was playing on the stereo and that there was a wonderful smell of lavender.

The bedrooms have been decorated with loving care by Mme Ganier – two have terraces. Colour schemes are bright and sunny – some are painted sunflower yellow, others a more subtle pale terracotta. There's some marbling effect on walls. Bathrooms – some have hand-made ceramic tiles from Salernes – are pretty; all are spotless and well-equipped.

The hotel is not in a pretty part of Vence, though.

Nearby Matisse chapel; Vence old town; Cannes (4 km).

Avenue Henri Giraud
06140 Vence
Tel 04 93 58 02 20
Fax 04 93 58 99 31
Location on outskirts of town in a garden
Meals breakfast only
Prices FF
Rooms 12 double; 5 with bath, 7 with shower; all with phone, TV, heating, minibar, hairdryer
Facilities swimming-pool; terrace, landscaped garden; car parking
Credit cards all
Children accepted
Disabled not possible
Pets accepted
Closed never
Proprietors M and Mme Ganier

The Rhône Valley

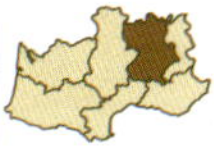

Converted hunting lodge, Beaulieu (Ardèche)

La Santoline

Residents of nearby villages still speak of the big, old, stone Santoline as "*le château*" – a reference to its 15thC origins. As time passed, it was used as a hunting lodge and remains a secluded place well off the beaten track. With no TV or other disruptions, there is little to disturb except the singing of birds and the occasional braying of a donkey. It is difficult to imagine a more relaxed setting. In the evenings, guests dine outside on the flower-filled terrace and watch the sun set behind the Cévennes.

Since opening their hotel in 1991, the Espenels have gathered a very loyal clientele by striking the right balance between easy-going conviviality and discreet attentiveness. Outsiders use the restaurant providing a menu of regional fare which changes daily, and affordable wines of the Ardèche. (The inside dining-room has a fine stone vaulted ceiling and tiled floor.) Bedrooms are pretty and simple in design, with much use of natural, rustic textures – tiled or pine floors, wicker furniture, some iron bedsteads, and white plastered walls. There are thick towels in the bathrooms. Most have exhilarating views of mountains.

Nearby Cave drawings in Vallon-Pont-d'Arc; Walking and river activities in the Gorges de l'Ardèche.

07460 Beaulieu
Tel 04 75 39 01 91
Fax 04 75 39 38 79
Location off D104 at La Croisée de Jalès, then D225; 2 km from Beaulieu
Meals all
Prices F-FF
Rooms 6 double and 1 suite; all with bath, phone, heating, minibar; 2 rooms with air-conditioning, rest with fans
Facilities pool; terrace; car parking
Credit cards MC, V
Children accepted
Disabled no special facilities
Pets accepted; 30F a day
Closed mid-Oct to end of March
Proprietors M and Mme Espenel

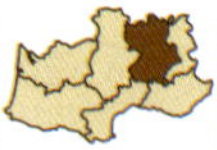

The Rhône Valley

Country-house hotel, Chonas-l'Amballan (Isère)

Domaine de Clairefontaine

A handsome 18thC house in splendid parkland – once the residence of the bishops of Lyon – this is one of two hotels just outside Vienne owned by the Girardons and is the one with the higher reputation for food and a Michelin star. (The other, Le Marais Saint-Jean, is nearby.)

This hotel is family-run and without pretension. Philippe Girardon specializes in a mixture of traditional and modern cuisine – among his classics are roast lobster, and lamb seasoned with rosemary. The pretty air-conditioned restaurant is painted yellow, has a beamed ceiling, flagged floor and French windows that open out on to a garden terrace. The comfortable and attractive bedrooms are offered at modest prices; all differ greatly in style and furnishing. The large double rooms are especially appealing, as they are bigger and better appointed than most higher-priced equivalents in lesser hotels. Hallways and bathrooms have a slightly faded look, but the overall mood is dignified and refined. Dressing-gowns may be needed here – the hotel still has that once common feature of the French hotel, the shared bathroom. Rooms in the annexe are more up-to-date.

Nearby Vienne (12 km); Lyon (40 km).

38121 Chonas-l'Amballan
Tel 04 74 58 81 52
Fax 04 74 58 80 93
Location small country estate E of the Rhône; with secure parking and garage
Meals all
Prices F
Rooms 16; 14 double, 2 suites; all with bath, phone, heating; 2 with TV; 3 with hairdryer
Facilities sitting-room; terrace; tennis; helipad
Credit cards AE, MC, V
Children accepted
Disabled no special facilities
Pets accepted
Closed Dec and Jan
Proprietor Philippe Girardon

The Rhône Valley

Town hotel, Lyon (Rhône)

La Tour Rose

Philippe Chavent is a Lyon chef with a Michelin star – and a Renaissance man. In St-Jean, the old quarter, he has re-created the atmosphere of the residences of the great Florentine bankers and merchants by turning a 17thC building into something extraordinary. There are 12 spectacular bedrooms, each designed to illustrate a period in the long history of Lyon's silk industry. One is decorated with Fortuny pleats, another with art deco patterns designed by Dufy, and all are draped, from floor to ceiling, in silk, taffeta, velvet and other textiles. (Bathrooms are modern, with stone floors and walls, and are fitted with shiny stainless-steel wash-basins.)

The heart of the hotel is a pink tower and there are balustraded galleries, ornamental ponds with waterfalls, and terraced gardens. The fireplace in the bar was rescued from a condemned château and there is an original 13thC wall of a *jeu de paume* (real tennis) court. Panelling in the bar comes from the law courts at Chambéry. The dining-room is in the 13thC chapel of what used to be a convent, with a cobbled terrace and fabulous glass extension which opens to the sky in summer.

Nearby old Lyon.

22 rue du Boeuf
69005 Lyon
Tel 04 78 37 25 90
Fax 04 78 42 26 02
Location in the heart of Vieux Lyon, with private parking
Meals all
Prices FFFF
Rooms 6 double and 6 suites; all with bath, shower, phone, heating, air-conditioning, TV, minibar, hairdryer
Facilities terraces; sitting-room; car parking
Credit cards AE, DC, MC, V
Children accepted
Disabled no special facilities
Pets accepted
Closed never
Proprietor Philippe Chavent

The Rhône Valley

Old coaching inn, Malataverne (Drôme)

La Domaine du Colombier

Meticulously restored and full of flowers and colour, this pleasing 14thC stone building, once a stopover for pilgrims on the road to Santiago de Compostela, remains an ideal base for travellers (largely due to its position near the *autoroute* yet in the countryside). With its vine-clad façade, stone staircases, tiled roof, wrought-iron railings and penchant for flowers, this hotel really feels it is on the road to the South.

Owner M Barette cooks with liberal doses of olives, *aïoli,* basil, capers and coriander. Wild flowers, gathered in the grounds, brighten every table and service is efficient and professional. When the weather is favourable (and the infamous mistral is not blowing) guests dine on the terrace, which is, again, packed with flowers and absolutely enchanting in the evening glow of lamplight. There is a large restaurant with a vaulted ceiling. Flowers appear everywhere, on the table-cloths, on curtains and bedspreads and wallpaper (floral fabrics and cane furniture are on sale in the hotel shop). Many rooms have plants, too. But most important, perhaps, Mme Barette is a charming hostess, who leaves guests feeling gratefully indulged.
Nearby Montélimar (10 km); Valence (50 km).

Route de Donzère
26780 Malataverne
Tel 04 75 90 86 86
Fax 04 75 90 79 40
Location on private estate; take Montélimar Sud exit off A7 to Malataverne, then N7
Meals all
Prices FF-FFF
Rooms 20 double and 4 suites; 23 with bath, 1 with shower; all with phone, sat TV, heating; hairdryer on request
Facilities swimming-pool; terrace; private car parking
Credit cards AE, DC, MC, V
Children accepted
Disabled no special facilities
Pets accepted; 50F a day
Closed 25th Nov to 8th Dec; 29th Jan to 11th Feb
Proprietors M and Mme Barette

The Rhône Valley

Converted castle, Le Poët-Laval (Drôme)

Les Hospitaliers

Readers continue to be impressed by this distinctive hotel, within the ramparts of a 13thC castle and in a dominating position above the perched medieval village of Le Poët-Laval (400 m). So do we.

The attractive old stone buildings were formerly part of a stronghold of the Knights of Malta. (The Maltese cross is the hotel's emblem.) From the pool and the terrace – where meals are served in fine weather – the views across wooded countryside to hills beyond are spectacular. The very comfortable sitting-room is – unusually – on the top floor and makes the best of this attribute. Owner M Morin was an art dealer and there are many original paintings in the bedrooms, as well as antique carved hardwood furniture. The restaurant also has an interesting collection of pictures. Tables are laid with fine china, white linen, and candles; service is hard to fault and the food is excellent. The menu changes daily. The welcome from the charming Morin family is warm and genuine. The eldest son, Bernard, cooks, using the freshest produce available. His younger brother is the *sommelier;* there's a comprehensive cellar. A delightful hotel that makes a lasting impression on all its guests.

Nearby Montélimar (20 km); Viviers (30 km), medieval town.

26160 Le Poët-Laval
Tel 04 75 46 22 32
Fax 04 75 46 49 99
Location on the summit of a medieval perched village 4 km W of Dieulefit, with parking
Meals all
Prices FF-FFF
Rooms 21 double; 20 with bath, 1 with shower; 3 family rooms, all with bath; all with phone and heating
Facilities bar; sitting-room; TV room; pool; terrace
Credit cards AE, DC, MC, V
Children accepted
Disabled no special facilities
Pets accepted; dog's meal 30F
Closed 15th Nov to 15th March
Proprietors M and Mme Morin

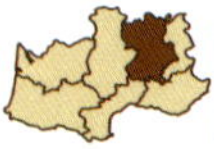

The Rhône Valley

Town hotel, Valence (Drôme)

Pic

The food's the thing here. Despite the death in 1992 of Jacques Pic, this remains (under son Alain) one of the best restaurants in the country with, at the last count, two Michelin stars – yet it is still delightfully modest. The big news *chez* Pic, however, has little to do with caviar and sea bass. It is that Alain and his charming sister, Anne-Sophie, have completely renovated the hotel that their grandfather opened so many years ago. Each of the existing five bedrooms has been updated with a smart new Provençal look and nine large rooms have been added.

And very attractive and stylish they are, too: marble-topped tables, damask upholstery, antique rugs, bathrooms in marble. Rooms are priced according to size, yet even the 'small' doubles are reasonably spacious. Some are very pretty; one has blue-and-white gingham wallpaper. The present generation of Pics devotes greater attention to the hotel, and it shows. What hasn't changed is the lovely terrace, pool and flower-filled garden. The few rooms at Pic were rarely vacant. Now there's more of a chance for those who wish to follow up their delicious – and expensive – Pic dinner with a copious Pic breakfast served in the room.
Nearby Vercors mountains; the Rhône.

285 Avenue Victor Hugo
26001 Valence
Tel 04 75 44 15 32
Fax 04 75 40 96 03
Location in town centre; private car parking
Meals all
Prices FFF-FFFF
Rooms 14 double; all with bath, phone, cable TV, heating, air-conditioning, minibar, hairdryer; most have safes
Facilities sitting-room; terrace; pool
Credit cards AE, DC, MC, V
Children accepted
Disabled 1 room
Pets accepted
Closed never
Proprietor Alain Pic

The Alps

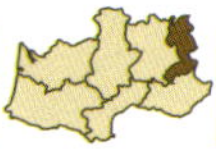

Chalet hotel, Manigod (Haute-Savoie)

Chalet Hôtel de la Croix-Fry

'Absolutely gorgeous' was the verdict of one of our reporters and a recent visit confirms the star rating of this wooden mountain chalet, at the highest point of an Alpine col, with a terrace overflowing with flowers. Run, with great pride, by a third generation of Veyrats – the chalet was once shared in the summer by the family and their cows – the hotel is cosy and welcoming. A wood fire burns on cool evenings and the sofas and armchairs gathered round the hearth are covered in sheepskin. The bedrooms are attractively rustic – even in the modern annexe-chalets, which provide adaptable family accommodation with kitchenettes. But what really impresses us is the evident pride of the family and their endless efforts to maximize a guest's stay. The Veyrats *love* running their hotel and the pleasure shows.

(In summer the family invite their guests to a picnic in the pastures with their cows; in winter the invitation is to ski.) The restaurant, serving nourishing mountain food, has spectacular views of peaks and valleys. Mme Guelpa-Veyrat's brother, Marc, is one of Savoie's culinary celebrities but the *tarte aux myrtilles* from her kitchen has many admirers.

Nearby Vallée de Manigod; Thônes (10 km); Annecy (26 km).

Rte du Col de la Croix-Fry
Manigod
74230 Thônes
Tel 04 50 44 90 16
Fax 04 50 44 94 87
Location on the col, 5 km NE of Manigod, on D16 6 km S of La Clusaz; garden and car parking
Meals all
Prices FF-FFFF+
Rooms 12 double with bath; all with heating, phone, sat TV; some with terrace or balcony
Facilities sitting-room; bar; heated swimming-pool; gymnastics room; tennis
Credit cards AE, MC, V
Children accepted
Disabled no special facilities
Pets not accepted
Closed 15th Sept to 15th Dec; 15th April to 15th June
Proprietor Mme Marie-Ange Guelpa-Veyrat

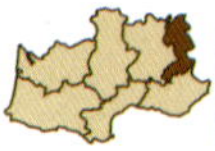

The Alps

Country-house hotel, La Rochette (Savoie)

Hostellerie Les Châtaigniers

French hotel brochures are normally illustrated with flattering soft-focus colour photographs. Les Châtaigniers is daringly different: black and white for them. And now we know why. 'It really was fun' said one visitor. Our inspector was likewise captivated. 'We don't have keys in the door, you are *chez vous*' was how he was greeted by his hostess, Mme Rey, who returned to her family home in 1991 from Paris (which she detests). With her came her philosopher partner, Philippe Romain, who trained as an actor, travelled widely and then became a chef. The house has the feel of a 19thC *salon* – Mme Recamier sprang to the mind of our inspector – with books and periodicals, in many languages, everywhere, and real paintings.

Between courses, philosopher-chef M Romain leaves his stove to discuss the world in general and may return after the cheese and salad to pick up on one of his favourite *bêtes noires*: modern cookery schools. The whole place buzzes with originality, character and life. Added to that, M Romain's food is wonderful and the setting of the late-19thC house, set off the road and in a large park, is most soothing. Spacious bathrooms come with comfortable beds.
Nearby Grenoble (47 km); Allevard (9 km); Chambéry (29 km).

Rue Maurice-Franck
73110 La Rochette
Tel 04 79 25 50 21
Fax 04 79 25 79 97
Location in a valley with mountain views; in large park with ample parking
Meals all (dinner obligatory)
Prices F-FF
Rooms 5; all with bath, phone; 2 with TV
Facilities swimming-pool; terrace; sitting-room with piano; games room; library
Credit cards all
Children accepted (if well behaved)
Disabled no special facilities
Pets not welcome
Closed 1st to 16th Jan
Proprietor Mme Rey

Bordeaux and the Dordogne

Town hotel, Astaffort

Le Square

The Cabrels – Philippe is the brother of singer Francis Cabrel – have given a fresh, bright, new face to this traditional shuttered building on the square of a small town between Bordeaux and Toulouse. Bedrooms are large with modern paintings. A beamed dining-room looks out to colourful ceramics on terrace.

■ 5, place de la Craste, 47220 Astaffort (Lot-et-Garonne) **Tel** 05 53 47 20 40 **Fax** 05 53 47 10 38 **Meals** all **Prices** F-FF **Rooms** 8; with bath or shower; all with phone, TV, air-conditioning, heating, minibar, hairdryer **Credit cards** AE, MC, V **Closed** undecided

Village hotel, Beynac

Hotel Bonnet

This slightly faded beauty is one of a dying breed of affordable and old-fashioned roadside hotels. Décor is a throwback to earlier times, but rooms are clean and comfortable and there's a pleasing veranda and terrace for meals. Rooms with views of the Dordogne and four châteaux. Very friendly, helpful staff.

■ 24220 Beynac (Dordogne) **Tel** 05 53 29 50 01 **Fax** 05 53 29 83 74 **Meals** all **Prices** F **Rooms** 20 double; 18 with bath, 2 with shower; all with phone, heating; hairdryer on request **Credit cards** AE, DC, MC, V **Closed** never

Farmhouse hotel, Le Bugue

Auberge du Noyer

An enormous walnut tree gives this formerly ruined 18thC stone farmhouse its name. Paul and Jenny Dyer, English emigrés, have turned the ruins into a winningly attractive, relaxed and tranquil inn, with rustic rooms, beams, and exposed stone walls.

■ Le Reclaud de Bouny Bas, 24260 Le Bugue (Dordogne) **Tel** 05 53 07 11 73 **Fax** 05 53 54 57 44 **Meals** breakfast; dinner **Prices** F-FF **Rooms** 10 doubles; all with bath, shower, phone, heating **Credit cards** MC, V **Closed** 1st Nov-Easter

Restaurant with rooms, Cardaillac

Chez Marcel

M Marcel's bistro is in the heart of a picturesque medieval village and has checked table-cloths, lace curtains and well-priced traditional cuisine. Upstairs are tidy, clean rooms, with antique furniture. Guests all share one lavatory and shower (spotless) in the hallway.

■ Rue du 11 Mai 1944, 46100 Cardaillac (Lot) **Tel** 05 65 40 11 16 **Meals** all **Prices** F **Rooms** 6 double; with heating **Credit cards** none **Closed** never

Bordeaux and the Dordogne

Wine château, Castelnau-de-Médoc

Château du Foulon

The engaging M and Mme de Baritault du Carpia have opened up their elegant home in the heart of the Médoc for bed-and-breakfast guests. Bedrooms have beautiful antiques and the grounds are magnificent; there are swans on the lake and peacocks on the lawn.

■ 33480 Castelnau-de-Médoc (Gironde) **Tel** 05 56 58 20 18 **Fax** 05 56 58 23 43 **Meals** breakfast **Prices** F-FF **Rooms** 5; all with bath **Credit cards** not accepted **Closed** never

Country house hotel, Castillon-la-Bataille

Hostellerie du Château Lardier

A new owner took over this ivy-covered stone house in 1996 soon after it had been completely redecorated. It stands on a little hill with pleasant views of Bordeaux vineyards. Rooms are well-appointed with period bedsteads and marble-topped tables. The pool and terrace are very quiet. Good value.

■ Route de Sauveterre, Ruch, 33350 Castillon-la-Bataille (Gironde) **Tel** 05 57 40 54 11 **Fax** 05 57 40 70 38 **Meals** all **Prices** F-FF **Rooms** 10 double; 4 with bath, 6 with shower; all with phone, sat TV, heating, minibar **Credit cards** MC, V **Closed** 15th Dec-end Feb

Village inn, Dégagnac

Auberge sans Frontière

Mme Planche has lowered her rates at her modest little auberge in this quiet town. Rooms are on the small side, but bright and tidy, with showers and lavatories located in the hallway. The restaurant provides good, no-nonsense fare at reasonable prices.

■ Dégagnac, 46340 Salviac (Lot) **Tel** 05 65 41 52 88 **Meals** all **Prices** F **Rooms** 8 double; all with heating **Credit cards** MC, V **Closed** never

Village hotel, Domme

Hôtel de l'Esplanade

In a busy tourist village with splendid views over the Dordogne, this three-fireplace Logis is well furnished with taste and flair. Housekeeping is immaculate, service efficient. Some bedrooms and the terrace have superb views; some rooms are in an annexe. Michelin-starred cooking. Difficult car parking.

■ 24250 Domme (Dordogne) **Tel** 05 53 28 31 41 **Fax** 05 53 28 49 92 **Meals** all **Prices** FF **Rooms** 25; all with bath or shower, heating, phone, TV, hairdryer **Credit cards** AE, MC, V **Closed** 1st Nov-14th Feb

Bordeaux and the Dordogne

Village hotel, Les Eyzies-de-Tayac

Les Glycines

A handsome wisteria-covered house, in beautiful gardens, Les Glycines has unremarkable bedrooms, but an attractive terrace and dining-room. Some of the rooms are in an annexe. There's a swimming-pool and ample parking.

■ 24620 Les Eyzies-de-Tayac (Dordogne) **Tel** 05 53 06 97 07 **Fax** 05 53 06 92 19 **Meals** all **Prices** F-FF **Rooms** 25 double; all with bath or shower; all rooms have heating, phone **Credit cards** AE, MC, V **Closed** Nov-Easter

Town hotel, Les Eyzies-de-Tayac

Le Moulin de la Beune

This charming old mill, set beside a stream and far removed from the village bustle, offers extremely good value accommodation and food. Rooms are prettily furnished; bathrooms are spotless. The atmosphere is relaxed and the terrace is delightful.

■ 24620 Les Eyzies-de-Tayac (Dordogne) **Tel** 05 53 06 94 33 **Fax** 05 53 06 98 06 **Meals** all **Prices** F **Rooms** 20 double; 14 with bath, 6 with shower; all with phone and heating **Credit cards** AE, MC, V **Closed** 15th Nov-1st April

Village hotel, Gluges

Hôtel les Falaises

This good-value family-run Logis enjoys an enviable position – huddled below a fine cliff, on the edge of a tiny medieval village beside the Dordogne – with a restful garden. Bedrooms are simple, light and well decorated.

■ Gluges, 46600 Martel (Lot) **Tel** 05 65 37 33 59 **Fax** 05 65 37 34 19 **Meals** all **Prices** F **Rooms** 15, all with bath or shower, heating, phone **Credit cards** MC, V **Closed** Dec-Feb

Riverside hotel, Lalinde

Le Château

His reputation for cooking superb regional cuisine established, Guy Gensou has turned to the building – an extraordinary little turreted affair, jutting out over the Dordogne; bedrooms and bathrooms have been refurbished and a cosy new sitting area designed. Some of the bathrooms are in round towers. Pool.

■ Rue de Verdun, 24150 Lalinde (Dordogne) **Tel** 05 61 01 82 **Fax** 05 53 24 74 60 **Meals** all **Prices** FF **Rooms** 7 double; 4 with bath, 3 with shower; all with phone, TV, heating, hairdryer **Credit cards** AE, DC, MC, V **Closed** Jan; third week Sept

Bordeaux and the Dordogne

Country guest-house, Lascabanes

La Petite Auberge

At M and Mme Duler's captivating *maison d'hôtes* guests make themselves at home and dine together at a long table. Much of the appeal lies in the knowledge that this is a working farm, with boar, pigs, ducks, and vegetables in the *potager* (all used in Mme's cooking). Rooms are rustic and comfortable. Pool.

■ Domaine de St-Géry, 46800 Lascabanes (Lot) **Tel** 05 65 31 82 51 **Fax** 05 65 22 92 89 **Meals** breakfast, dinner **Prices** F **Rooms** 4 and 1 suite; all with bath, phone **Credit cards** MC, V **Closed** 10th Jan-15th March

Country inn, Laveyssière

Auberge de la Devinière

Roses climb the walls of this gabled 18thC inn set deep in the heart of the Périgord countryside. There are antiques and floral fabrics throughout and many rooms have angled ceilings, beams and dormer windows. Meals are good – everything from croissants to *foie gras* is made on the premises. Pool, terrace

■ Pas de l'Eyraud, 24130 Laveyssière (Dordogne) **Tel** 05 53 81 66 43 **Fax** 05 53 81 54 44 **Meals** all **Prices** FF **Rooms** 7 double; 3 with bath, 4 with shower; all with phone, TV, heating, hairdryer **Credit cards** MC, V **Closed** 20th Oct-10th Nov

Country house, Loubressac

Château de Gamot

M and Mme Belliers, a Parisian couple, have recently opened their 16thC summer residence as a charming bed-and-breakfast. Set on a 50-hectare wooded estate, there's a pool and private parking. Rooms are well-appointed, but with few creature comforts.

■ 46130 Loubressac (Lot) **Tel** 05 65 38 58 50 **Meals** breakfast only **Prices** F; breakfast included **Rooms** 4; 2 with private bath, 2 with shared bath **Credit cards** none **Closed** 1st Nov-1st May

Country hotel, Razac d'Eymet

La Petite Auberge

Opened by its English owners in 1990, but run in a thoroughly French style, this converted farm – set in tranquil open countryside south of Bergerac – retains an informal 'family' atmosphere and is popular with foreign tourists and locals. Comfortable bedrooms. Outdoor giant chess set, swimming-pool.

■ 24500 Razac d'Eymet (Dordogne) **Tel** 05 53 24 69 27 **Fax** 05 53 27 33 55 **Meals** all **Prices** F **Rooms** 7, all with heating, phone **Credit cards** MC, V **Closed** restaurant only Sun and Mon

Bordeaux and the Dordogne

Town hotel, Ribérac

Hôtel de France

A classic two-fireplace Logis de France – an old flower-decked inn at the heart of a bustling market town, with a pretty and warmly inviting restaurant and modest but spacious bedrooms which can accomodate families. Excellent value.

■ 3 rue Marc Dufraisse, 24600 Ribérac (Dordogne) **Tel** 05 53 90 00 61 **Fax** 05 53 91 06 05 **Meals** all **Prices** F **Rooms** 20; all with bath or shower, phone **Credit cards** MC, V **Closed** never

Country inn, Rocamadour

Les Vieilles Tours

Even the smallest rooms in this beautifully-restored stone building, dating from the 13thC and 17thC, are spacious and bright. The sitting-room is in a turret wing. Views across open countryside are uninterrupted. Mme Zozzoli cooks. Pool.

■ Lafage, 46500 Rocamadour (Lot) **Tel** 05 65 33 68 01 **Fax** 05 65 33 68 59 **Meals** all **Prices** F-FF **Rooms** 9 double, 9 family; 17 with bath, 1 with shower; all have phone, heating; some with TV **Credit cards** AE, MC, V **Closed** 12th Nov-end March

Riverside hotel, La Roque-Gageac

La Plume d'Oie

Four comfortable bedrooms have been added to this attractive little highly-acclaimed restaurant in a pretty village on the Dordogne river. The rooms at the front are on the road and may be a little noisy, but all are charmingly, yet simply, decorated.

■ 24250 La Roque Gageac (Dordogne) **Tel** 05 53 29 57 05 **Fax** 05 53 31 04 81 **Meals** all **Prices** F **Rooms** 4 double; all with bath, shower, phone, TV, heating, minibar **Credit cards** MC, V **Closed** Feb

Country guesthouse, St-Avit

Le Moulin de St-Avit

The English hosts at this clean, efficient and reliable converted mill in a very pretty secluded 'classified' valley are attentive and friendly. It is rural rather than rustic, with pine furniture. Rooms are rather small. Pool and horses.

■ 47150 Gavaudun (Lot-et-Garonne) **Tel** 05 53 40 86 80 **Fax** 05 53 40 98 20 **Meals** breakfast only **Prices** F **Rooms** 5; 4 double, 1 single; all with shower and WC; Goldfinch room for disabled **Credit cards** MC, V **Closed** Nov-Easter

Bordeaux and the Dordogne

Village inn, St-Cirq-Lapopie

Auberge du Sombral

Mme has been known to give a cool reception, but there is much to like about this beautifully restored house in the heart of a lovely – but much visited – medieval village. Food and housekeeping are excellent. There's a small terrace. But there is no car parking within the town walls; heavy baggage is a problem.

■ St-Cirq-Lapopie, 46330 Cabrerets (Lot) **Tel** 05 65 31 26 08 **Fax** 05 65 30 26 37 **Meals** all **Prices** F **Rooms** 10 double; 5 with bath, 5 with shower; most with phone, heating **Credit cards** MC, V **Closed** 15th Nov-1st April

Town hotel, St-Cyprien

L'Abbaye

This unpretentious, friendly place has a captivating atmosphere. In the rustic, stone-flagged sitting-room you can see the old pastry oven. The best bedrooms (first floor of new annexe) are spacious and attractive. There's a terrace, pool and car parking.

■ Rue de l'Abbaye, 24220 St-Cyprien (Dordogne) **Tel** 05 53 29 20 48 **Fax** 05 53 29 15 85 **Meals** all **Prices** FF **Rooms** 24 double; 15 with bath, 9 with shower; all with phone, heating; some with hairdryer; TV on request **Credit cards** AE, MC, V **Closed** 15th Oct-15th April

Fishing lodge, St-Merd-de-Lapleau

Au Rendez-Vous des Pêcheurs

Lost deep in the woods along a particularly isolated stretch of the Dordogne, this fishing lodge serves up excellent fresh fish and *foie gras* in the surprisingly elegant dining-room and offers inexpensive, comfortable rooms. Friendly welcome; car parking.

■ Pont du Chambon, 19320 St-Merd-de-Lapleau (Corrèze) **Tel** 05 55 27 88 39 **Fax** 05 55 27 83 19 **Meals** all **Prices** F **Rooms** 8 double; 6 with bath, 2 with shower; all with phone, TV, heating **Credit cards** MC, V **Closed** 11th Nov-end Jan

Village inn, St-Robert

La Maison Anglaise

La patronne, as the name suggests, is English: Dawn Clarke opened her hotel eight years ago and her casual friendliness endears both travellers and locals. Rooms are large, and rustic, with creaking floorboards and duvets on the beds. Restaurant, terrace, superb views, pool.

■ Le Bourg, St-Robert, 19310 Ayen (Corrèze) **Tel** 05 55 25 19 58 **Fax** 05 55 25 23 00 **Meals** all **Prices** F **Rooms** 6 double; all with shower, heating, tea- and coffee-making facilities; hairdryer on request **Credit cards** AE, MC, V **Closed** 25th Dec-end Jan

Country hotel, Sarlat

Hostellerie de Meysset

'Splendid room, very good food, pleasant owners, good views,' runs a reader's report on this creeper-covered, typical Périgord country-house. Its style is traditional and unpretentious, though not without floral excesses. The food leans towards traditional regional elements, too.

■ Route des Eyzies, 24299 Sarlat (Dordogne) **Tel** 05 53 59 08 29 **Fax** 05 53 28 47 61 **Meals** all **Prices** FF **Rooms** 26 double; 22 with bath, 4 with shower; all with phone, heating **Credit cards** AE, DC, MC, V **Closed** 10th Oct-15th April

Medieval manor, Vézac

Manoir de Rochecourbe

No need to worry that this old favourite will close, as we had once feared: it has merely passed from one generation of the Roger family to another. A round tower housing the staircase gives the house a touch of grandeur. Large bedrooms have beams and enormous fireplaces; many have a view of the nearby château.

■ 24220 Vézac (Dordogne) **Tel** 05 53 31 09 84 **Fax** 05 53 28 59 07 **Meals** breakfast **Prices** F-FF **Rooms** 6 double; 5 with bath, 1 with shower; all with phone, heating; hairdryer on request **Credit cards** AE, DC, MC, V **Closed** 12th Nov-end of March

Medieval inn, Cordes (The South-West)

Hostellerie du Vieux Cordes

A genuinely medieval building in a popular 13thC fortified village, this has a delightful open courtyard, shaded by a twisted wisteria. Bedrooms are modern and the quietest look out over open countryside. Part of the Yves Thuriès domain.

■ Rue St-Michel, 81170 Cordes-sur-Ciel (Tarn) **Tel** 05 63 56 00 12 **Fax** 05 63 56 02 47 **Meals** all **Prices** F-FF **Rooms** 21; 7 with bath, 14 with shower; all with phone, TV, heating **Credit cards** AE, MC, V **Closed** Jan

Restaurant with rooms, Hossegor (The South-West)

Les Huitrières du Lac

Primarily a restaurant, specializing (as you might expect) in fish and seafood – though there are alternatives. The larger dining-room and the best bedrooms share a view over the adjacent lake. Bedrooms are plain but spacious; some have balconies. Pleasant setting; value for money.

■ 1187 Avenue du Touring Club, 40150 Hossegor (Landes) **Tel** 05 58 43 51 48 **Fax** 05 58 41 73 11 **Meals** all **Prices** F **Rooms** 9; all with bath, central heating, phone **Credit cards** AE, MC, V **Closed** Jan to early Feb

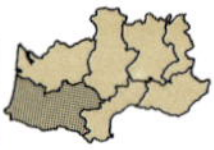

The South-West

Country hotel, Montfort-en-Chalosse

Aux Tauzins

A solid Logis in its third generation of family ownership, this is a very comfortable, pleasant hotel with white walls and green shutters and excellent views over countryside. Rooms are bright and fair value for family use. Wisteria-shaded terrace and pool.

■ Route d'Hagetmau, 40380 Montfort-en-Chalosse (Landes) **Tel** 05 58 98 60 22 **Fax** 05 58 98 61 09 **Meals** all **Prices** F **Rooms** 16; 7 with bath, 9 with shower; all with phone, sat TV, heating **Credit cards** MC, V **Closed** 1st-15th Oct; mid-end Jan

Village hotel, Plaisance

Le Ripa Alta

A comfortable, unfussy village hotel whose reputation rests on veteran owner Maurice Coscuella, who trained alongside Bocuse and Troisgros. Bedrooms are adequate (one with balcony) and quiet, except Saturday nights when the nearby disco is on.

■ 3 place de l'Église, 32160 Plaisance (Gers) **Tel** 05 62 69 30 43 **Fax** 05 62 69 36 99 **Meals** all **Prices** F-FF **Rooms** 14 and 1 suite; 10 with bath; all with phone, heating; some with TV, hairdryer **Credit cards** AE, MC, V **Closed** never

Farmhouse hotel, Pont-de-l'Arn

La Métairie Neuve

The Métairie is a tastefully renovated old farm with its heritage properly respected – exposed beams, stone walls, polished tiled floors – and a relaxed atmosphere. Mme Tournier is a charming hostess who keeps the antique-furnished public areas looking immaculate.

■ Pont-de-l'Arn, 81660 Mazamet (Tarn) **Tel** 05 63 61 23 31 **Fax** 05 63 61 94 75 **Meals** all **Prices** F-FF **Rooms** 11; all with bath, central heating, phone, TV **Credit cards** DC, MC, V **Closed** 15th Dec-20th Jan

Country hotel, Projan

Château de Projan

The friendly and welcoming Vichets have given their restored château an artistic character by mixing work by modern painters with antiques of all ages. Bathroom facilities are not good here – there's a block of showers and WCs on the top floor – but improvements are on the way. Interesting ambience.

■ 32400 Projan (Gers) **Tel** 05 62 09 46 21 **Fax** 05 62 09 44 08 **Meals** all; for residents by reservation **Prices** F-FF **Rooms** 11; some with shower; all with phone, heating; TV on request **Credit cards** all major **Closed** Dec and Jan

The South-West

Country hotel, Sabres

Auberge des Pins

An excellent example of unpretentious French hotelkeeping – a three-fireplace Logis in a chalet-style building offering satisfactory accommodation and food in well-cared-for surroundings at moderate prices. The restaurant caters as much to locals as to travellers.

■ Route de la Piscine, 40630 Sabres (Landes) **Tel** 05 58 07 50 47 **Fax** 05 58 07 56 74 **Meals** all **Prices** F-FF **Rooms** 24, all with bath or shower, central heating, phone, cable TV **Credit cards** AE, V **Closed** Jan

Seaside hotel, St-Jean-de-Luz

La Devinière

Discreet, refined, unusual, beautifully furnished, little hotel in a pedestrianised street, run by a former lawyer and an antique dealer. (Stanislav Richter stayed here and it is named after Rabelais' house.) Pretty little garden; parking nearby.

■ 5, rue Loquin, 64500 St-Jean-de-Luz (Pyrénées-Atlantiques) **Tel** 05 59 26 05 51 **Fax** 05 59 51 26 38 **Meals** breakfast only **Prices** FF **Rooms** 8; all with bath, phone, heating; hairdryer on request **Credit cards** MC, V **Closed** last 2 weeks Nov

Seaside hotel, St-Jean-de-Luz

La Fayette

This little family-run hotel occupies a prime spot in the pedestrianised heart of the animated port and resort of St-Jean. The building is in Dutch style, all arches and red brick, and it has a street terrace for outside meals. Small, simple but cheerful bedrooms.

■ 18-20 rue de la République, 64500 St-Jean-de-Luz (Pyrénées-Atlantiques) **Tel** 05 59 26 17 74 **Fax** 05 59 51 11 78 **Meals** all **Prices** F **Rooms** 18; all with central heating, phone, TV **Credit cards** AE, DC, MC, V **Closed** never

Country spa hotel, Sevignac-Meyrac

Les Bains de Secours

Uncompromisingly rustic Logis – a renovated old farm with rough, wooden wall-panelling, paved floors and no frills. Good country cuisine. Complete peace and calm; nearby is a small private spa with sulphur springs and steam bath dating back to the 18thC.

■ 64260 Sevignac-Meyrac (Pyrénées-Atlantiques) **Tel** 05 59 05 62 11 **Fax** 05 59 05 76 56 **Meals** all **Prices** F **Rooms** 5 and 2 family; most with shower; all with phone, TV, heating, hairdryer **Credit cards** AE, DC, MC, V **Closed** no fixed date

The South-West/Languedoc-Roussillon

Country villa, Soustons

La Bergerie

Mme Clavier has made her immaculate whitewashed house – built in southern single-storey style – a calm and civilized haven where the slow pace of life is infectious. The (obligatory) set dinner is based on whatever is fresh and good at the time. The bedrooms look on to neat gardens.

■ Avenue du Lac, 40140 Soustons (Landes) **Tel** 05 58 41 11 43 **Meals** breakfast, dinner **Prices** F **Rooms** 12; all with bath, central heating, phone **Credit cards** DC, MC, V **Closed** Nov-Mar

Town hotel, Toulouse

Hôtel des Beaux Arts

Close to the École des Beaux Arts, this elegant listed 18thC building on the banks of the Garonne has been a hotel for 100 years and has just been completely – and smartly – renovated. At street level is the Brasserie des Beaux Arts, a lively, very French, eating-place. Parking.

■ 1, place du Pont Neuf, 31000 Toulouse (Haute-Garonne) **Tel** 05 61 23 40 50 **Fax** 05 61 22 02 27 **Meals** breakfast only; other meals in Brasserie **Prices** FF-FFFF **Rooms** 19; 17 with bath, 2 with shower; all with phone, sat TV, heating, air-conditioning, minibar **Closed** never

Country hotel, Valence-sur-Baïse

La Ferme de Flaran

The hotel – a former farmhouse belonging to the nearby 12thC Cistercian abbey – is the creation of Mme Manet (of the Trois Lys, Condom) and bears her hallmark of professionalism, style and charm. The restaurant is well above average – attractive outside dining area. (Some traffic noise in front rooms.) Pool.

■ 32310 Valence-sur-Baïse (Gers) **Tel** 05 62 28 58 22 **Fax** 05 62 28 56 89 **Meals** all **Prices** F **Rooms** 14; all with bath or shower, phone, heating; hairdryer on request **Credit cards** MC, V **Closed** 1st-31st Jan; 1 week in Oct

Town hotel, Aigues-Mortes

Hôtel Les Arcades

In this architectural gem of a little town, a handsome listed 16thC house owned by the obliging Merquiol family offers beamed and chandeliered rooms over their restaurant. The original stone staircase leads up to marble fireplaces and gilt mirrors.

■ 23 Bld Gambetta, 30220 Aigues-Mortes (Gard) **Tel** 04 66 53 81 13 **Fax** 04 66 53 75 46 **Meals** all **Prices** F **Rooms** 6 double; 5 with bath; all with phone, TV, air-conditioning **Credit cards** all **Closed** 12th-28th Nov and 11th-27th Feb

Languedoc-Roussillon

Town hotel, Aigues-Mortes

Hotel Les Templiers

This 17thC town house was rescued from ruin five years ago and lovingly restored to become a smart little hotel. Painted furniture and Provençal fabrics abound. A pretty paved garden to the rear and a free secure garage are added perks.

■ 23 rue de la Republique, 30220 Aigues-Mortes (Gard)**Tel** 04 66 53 66 56 **Fax** 04 66 53 69 61 **Meals** breakfast; omelettes and salad **Prices** FF **Rooms** 11 double; 7 with bath, 4 with shower; all with phone, TV, air-conditioning **Credit cards** all **Closed** Nov-Feb

Seaside hotel, Argelès-sur-Mer

Le Cottage

An efficient, bright, modern holiday hotel, with a young, charming *patronne*, this is in a quiet, residential part of the town, with a large swimming-pool and garden, and lots of green, white and yellow inside. Very comfortable, with excellent dining facilities, inside and out.

■ 21 rue Arthur-Rimbaud, 66703 Argelès-sur-Mer (Pyrénées-Orientales) **Tel** 04 68 81 07 33 **Fax** 04 68 81 59 69 **Meals** all **Prices** F-FF **Rooms** 32 double; 20 with bath, 12 with shower, all with phone, TV, heating, hairdryer **Credit cards** MC, V **Closed** 1st Nov-31st Mar

Country house hotel, Carcassonne

Domaine d'Auriac

A relaxing country house where the attractions are mainly outdoors: golf and tennis on the doorstep, a pool surrounded by beautifully manicured gardens, and a dining terrace with serene and verdant views. Comfortable inside, too. A Relais & Châteaux.

■ Route de St-Hilaire, 11009 Carcassonne (Aude) **Tel** 04 68 25 72 22 **Fax** 04 68 47 35 54 **Meals** all **Prices** FFF-FFFF **Rooms** 25; all with bath or shower, heating, phone, TV, minibar **Credit cards** AE, DC, MC, V **Closed** 8th Jan-2nd Feb

Hilltop village hotel, Castillon-du-Gard

Le Vieux Castillon

This is a conventional, expensive four-star, one Michelin star, Relais & Châteaux, offering comfort and a surprise: it is a cluster of houses in a restored medieval village. A street runs through it. Sleep in a vaulted bedroom; dine in a cloister. There's a swimming-pool, too.

■ Castillon-du-Gard, 30210 Remoulins **Tel** 04 66 37 00 77 **Fax** 04 66 37 28 17 **Meals** all **Prices** FFF-FFFF **Rooms** 35, all with bath, phone, TV, air-conditioning, minibar **Credit cards** all **Closed** Jan and Feb

Country hotel, La Favède

Auberge Cévenole

Although the approach through an industrialized valley is disagreeable, this small hotel has an above-average garden, fine views and is a haven of peace and calm. Bedrooms and bathrooms range from adequate to very comfortable. Pool.

■ La Favède, 30110 Les-Salles-du-Gardon (Gard) **Tel** 04 66 34 12 13 **Fax** 04 66 34 50 50 **Meals** all **Prices** F-FF **Rooms** 19 double; all with bath or shower; all have heating, phone. **Credit cards** MC, V **Closed** mid-Oct-Mar.

Country hotel, St-Pierre-dels-Forcats

Mouli del Riu

St-Pierre is in one of the Pyrenees' major ski areas, around Font Romeu. The Mouli – a modern and undistinguished house, despite the traditional-sounding name – is a simple and rather quirky place. We've had no reason to doubt the place since it entered the guide in 1989, but it has been in new hands since 1992. More reports, please.

■ St-Pierre-dels-Forcats, 66210 Mont-Louis (Pyrénées-Orientales) **Tel** 04 68 04 20 36 **Fax** 04 68 04 20 25 **Meals** all **Prices** F **Rooms** 15, all with bath, central heating **Credit cards** AE, MC, V **Closed** Wed; Nov-mid-Dec

Restaurant with rooms, Tavel

Hostellerie du Seigneur

This congenial little restaurant-with-rooms is a cosy place, with a pleasant little terrace overlooking a square. Inside a bar-cum-reception area leads into the hotel's hub: an intimate stone-vaulted dining-room where *cuisine bourgeoise* is offered. Bedrooms are old-fashioned, but entirely adequate.

■ Place du Seigneur, 30126 Tavel (Gard) **Tel** 04 66 50 04 26 **Meals** all **Prices** F **Rooms** 7, with heating **Credit cards** MC, V **Closed** mid-Dec-mid-Jan

Town hotel, Villeneuve-lès-Avignon

La Magnaneraie

Pricey and often busy with functions, this four-star hotel has a classically-inspired garden, a swimming-pool, and a *trompe l'oeil* in the dining-room. The food is said to be among the best in the Gard – chef Gérard Prayal is a Maître Cuisiner de France.

■ 37 rue Camp de Bataille, 30400 Villeneuve-lès-Avignon (Gard) **Tel** 04 90 25 11 11 **Fax** 04 90 25 46 37 **Meals** all **Prices** FFF-FFFF **Rooms** 29; all with bath, phone, sat TV, air-conditioning, heating, minibar **Credit cards** all **Closed** never

Auvergne & the Massif Central

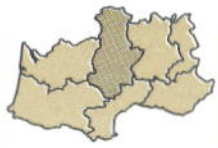

Country house hotel, Boisset

Auberge de Concasty

With rooms named after wild flowers and the cattle of *le patron* in the pasture, this remote, pretty *auberge* radiates country charm. Mme cooks unpretentious Franco-Auvergnat dishes. Gym; sauna; whirlpool bath; swimming-pool; donkeys.

■ 15600 Boisset (Cantal) **Tel** 04 71 62 21 16 **Fax** 04 71 62 22 22
Meals all **Prices** F-FF **Rooms** 16; all with bath, phone, TV
Credit cards all major **Closed** 15th-30th Nov; Jan

Manor house hotel, Champagnac

Château de Lavendes

Remotely situated among hill farms, this well-kept family-run manor house dates back to the 14thC. Chef/owner Gérard Gimmig is one of Paul Bocuse's Eurotoques and wins awards for his puddings. Swimming-pool, park, terrace.

■ 15350 Champagnac (Cantal) **Tel** 04 71 69 62 79 **Fax** 04 71 63 65 33
Meals all **Prices** FF **Rooms** 8 double; 4 with bath, 4 with shower; all with phone, TV **Credit cards** all **Closed** 15th Nov-1st Mar

Village inn, Montsalvy

Auberge Fleurie

The two attractive dining-rooms – polished wood dressers, gleaming copper, red-check table-cloths – are the focal point of this delightful creeper-covered *auberge*. Rooms look on to a main road; half the hotel is taken up by a busy *café tabac*.

■ Place du Barry, 15120 Montsalvy (Cantal) **Tel** 04 71 49 20 02
Meals all **Prices** F **Rooms** 11; all with central heating
Credit cards AE, DC, MC, V **Closed** restaurant only mid-Jan-mid-Feb

Manor house hotel, St-Martin-Valmeroux

Hostellerie de la Maronne

This Belgian-owned 19thC country house in a peaceful valley in the Auvergne has large, well-equipped rooms, all with bath, and a warm and friendly atmosphere. Food – 'French, eclectic' – is taken seriously; Mme is in charge. Tennis court, pool, lift.

■ Le Theil, 15140 St-Martin-Valmeroux (Cantal) **Tel** 04 71 69 20 33
Fax 04 71 69 28 22 **Meals** all **Prices** FF **Rooms** 21 double, all with bath; all with heating, phone, minibar; some with balcony or terrace
Credit cards AE MC V **Closed** Nov-Mar

Château hotel, St-Saturnin-de-Lenne

Château Saint Saturnin

This château, on which work began in 1778 for the Vicomte de Campagnac, was, at the turn of the century, transformed into an art deco showpiece by a Parisian restaurateur. Recently restored by an Anglo-American couple, it is now a sumptuous country house hotel, with formal park and high-quality *cuisine.* Pool.

■ 12650 St-Saturnin-de-Lenne (Aveyron) **Tel** 05 65 70 36 00 **Fax** 05 65 70 36 19 **Meals** breakfast and dinner **Prices** FF-FFF **Rooms** 8; all with bath, phone, heating; TV, hairdryer on request **Credit cards** all except AE **Closed** 5th/6th Jan-Easter

Riverside hotel, St-Sernin-sur-Rance

Hôtel Carayon

The Carayons have become almost too successful for our guide – their hotel now has an astounding 60 rooms and a terrace to take 250 covers. But the professionalism and quality remains just the same. Excellent food from Pierre Carayon's kitchen.

■ Place du Fort, 12380 St-Sernin-sur-Rance (Aveyron) **Tel** 05 65 99 60 26 **Fax** 05 65 99 69 26 **Meals** all **Prices** F-FF **Rooms** 60; all with bath or shower; all with phone, sat TV, heating, minibar, hairdryer **Credit cards** AE, DC, MC, V **Closed** 4 weeks in Nov

Château hotel, Target

Château de Boussac

The moated château has Louis XV antiques in the reception rooms, an ornamental lake and formal gardens. It is the home of the Marquis and Marquise de Longeuil – he works in overalls on the estate by day and cooks at least one course of the evening meal.

■ Target, 03140 Chantelle (Allier) **Tel** 04 70 40 63 20 **Fax** 04 70 40 60 03 **Meals** breakfast, dinner **Prices** FF-FFFF **Rooms** 4 double, 2 suites; all with bath and central heating **Credit cards** AE MC V **Closed** Nov-Feb (except by reservation in advance)

Village inn, Vitrac

La Tomette

'This hotel has all the qualities of peace, welcome, attractive setting and very good food that characterize your selections,' a reader says of the Tomette – a jolly inn, much expanded and improved over the last 15 years, evidently without the loss of its essential appeal. Pleasant garden, pool.

■ 15220 Vitrac (Cantal) **Tel** 04 71 64 70 94 **Fax** 04 71 64 77 11 **Meals** all **Prices** F-FF **Rooms** 18; all with bath or shower, central heating, phone, TV **Credit cards** AE, MC, V **Closed** Jan to Mar

Converted castle, Les Arcs

Le Logis du Guetteur

This 11thC fort still looks more or less as it must have done nine centuries ago. The modernized bedrooms are quiet, with lovely views, and there is a pleasant pool. But the main emphasis is on the medieval cellar restaurant and terrace, where satisfying classic dishes are served.

■ Place du Château, 83460 Les Arcs (Var) **Tel** 04 94 73 30 82 **Fax** 04 73 39 95 **Meals** all **Prices** FF **Rooms** 11; all with bath or shower, central heating **Credit cards** AE, DC, MC, V **Closed** mid-Jan-mid-Feb

Town hotel, Arles

Hôtel Calendal

A 400-year-old nettle tree stands in the delightful garden of this elegant hotel recently created out of an 18thC building. Rooms, with painted Provençal furniture and many decorated in lavender blue and yellow, have garden views and new bathrooms.

■ 22, place Pomme, 13200 Arles (Bouches-du-Rhône) **Tel** 04 90 96 11 89 **Fax** 04 90 96 05 84 **Meals** breakfast; light lunch; *salon de thé* **Prices** F **Rooms** 27; most with bath; all with phone, heating, air-conditioning, sat TV, hairdryer **Credit cards** all **Closed** never

Town hotel, Arles

Grand Hôtel Nord-Pinus

An extravagant and imaginative renovation of Arles' old cult hotel in the Place du Forum has given it back its Bohemian past, with wrought-iron beds, gilded mirrors, and chandeliers. Picasso slept here. The yellow bar is a shrine to bullfighters. Garage.

■ Place du Forum, 13200 Arles (Bouches-du-Rhône) **Tel** 04 90 93 44 44 **Fax** 04 90 93 34 00 **Meals** all **Prices** FFF-FFFF **Rooms** 23; 22 with bath; all with phone, sat TV, heating, air-conditioning, minibar, hairdryer **Credit cards** all **Closed** never

Town hotel, Avignon

Hôtel de la Mirande

Arguably the most beautiful hotel in the south, the extravagantly restored Mirande – a historic monument – is exquisitely furnished and decorated in 18thC style with marble bathrooms and an inner courtyard. Inexpensive lunch menu.

■ 4, place de l'Amirande, 84000 Avignon **Tel** 04 90 85 93 93 **Fax** 04 90 86 26 85 **Meals** all **Prices** FFFF+ **Rooms** 20; all with bath, phone, cable TV, heating, air-conditioning, minibar, hairdryer, safe **Credit cards** all **Closed** never

Provence-Côte d'Azur

Village hotel, Le Barroux

Les Géraniums

At the entrance to a small, medieval village, M Roux's ever-expanding hotel has rather boring, uniform bedrooms – some in a block over the road – but continues to bring in compliments from readers. Large terrace; locked parking. Often busy with functions and groups.

■ 84330 Le Barroux (Vaucluse) **Tel** 04 90 62 41 06 **Fax** 04 90 62 56 48 **Meals** all **Prices** F **Rooms** 22; 8 with bath; all with phone, heating **Credit cards** all **Closed** Jan and Feb

Riverside hotel, Callas

Hostellerie les Gorges de Pennafort

At night, the lights of this elegant one-Michelin-star hotel illuminate the dramatic crags of the Pennafort gorges; there's a constant sound of running water. Luxury bedrooms; luxury prices.

■ 83830 Callas (Var) **Tel** 04 94 76 66 51 **Fax** 04 94 76 67 23 **Meals** all **Prices** FF-FFFF **Rooms** 16; most with bath; all with phone, sat TV, heating, air-conditioning, minibar **Credit cards** AE, MC **Closed** 15th Jan-15th Mar

Country hotel, Callian

Auberge du Puits Jaubert

The 16thC vaulted dining-room is where the sheep were kept in this remote, green-shuttered small family hotel at the end of a 3-km track. Good, simple food; dull bedrooms; delightful place. Garden; terrace; abundant greenery.

■ Route du Lac Fondurance, 83440 Callian (Var) **Tel** 04 94 76 44 48 **Meals** all **Prices** F **Rooms** 8; some with baths; some with terraces; all with heating **Credit cards** V **Closed** 15th Nov-15th Dec

Town hotel, Cap d'Antibes

Auberge la Gardiole

This modest pink-washed, friendly, family-run small hotel has bargain prices for the area, a charming terrace, but nasty brown carpets. Some rooms have little terraces. Street parking.

■ 74 Chemin de la Garoupe, 06160 Cap d'Antibes (Alpes Maritimes) **Tel** 04 93 61 35 03 **Fax** 04 93 67 61 87 **Meals** all **Prices** F-FF **Rooms** 16 double, 1 single, 1 family; most with bath; all with phone, TV, heating, minibar; some with air-conditioning **Credit cards** all **Closed** Nov-end-Feb

Provence-Côte d'Azur

Village hotel, Le Castellet

Castel Lumière

In an 18thC stone house – once owned by the Lumière brothers (inventors of the cinema) – in a medieval hilltop village, the hotel has views to the sea. Frilly interior; fairy lights in the courtyard; piped music; impressive food; reasonable prices.

■ Le Portail, 83330 Le Castellet (Var) **Tel** 04 94 32 62 20 **Fax** 04 94 32 70 33 **Meals** all **Rooms** 6 double; 3 with bath, 3 with shower; all with phone, TV, heating **Prices** F-FF **Credit cards** no AE or DC **Closed** Jan

Mountain hotel, Le Clos Sorel

Auberge du Clos Sorel

Mme Mercier gives a warm welcome at her old stone converted farmhouse in a little mountain village of wooden chalets, with spectacular views, pure, fresh air, and every comfort. Pool; log fires; terrace. Dinner by candle-light.

■ Les Molanès, 04400 Pra-Loup (Alpes-de-Haute-Provence) **Tel** 04 92 84 10 74 **Fax** 04 92 84 09 14 **Meals** all **Prices** FF-FFF **Rooms** 11 double; all with bath, phone, TV; some with balcony; 1 with open fireplace **Credit cards** MC, V **Closed** 1st Sept-15th Dec; 15th Apr-1st July

Village hotel, Cotignac

Lou Calen

The shady garden, dining terrace and pool are the key attractions of this shuttered house on the occasionally noisy village square of Cotignac. The house is furnished in a homely blend of antique and rustic styles, and bedrooms vary considerably in size, style and price. Cooking is simple, but hearty.

■ 1 Cours Gambetta, 83850 Cotignac (Var) **Tel** 04 94 04 60 40 **Fax** 04 94 04 76 64 **Meals** all **Prices** F-FF **Rooms** 16; all with bath or shower, central heating, phone, TV **Credit cards** AE, DC, MC, V **Closed** Jan-late Mar

Country hotel, Esparron de Verdon

Le Roumanin

Ten years ago there was only scrub where a small hotel now stands in an enchanting garden with a lake view. Owner Mme Tellier keeps things simple: she cooks in the evenings, lights oil lamps, has no fax. A swimming-pool is hidden amid the lavender. For nature lovers.

■ Chemin des Plèches, 04800 Esparron de Verdon (Alpes-de-Haute-Provence) **Tel** 04 92 77 15 91 **Meals** breakfast, dinner **Prices** F-FF **Rooms** 10; all with bath, phone, heating; some with terrace **Credit cards** not accepted **Closed** Nov-Mar.

Provence-Côte d'Azur

Château hotel, Eygalières

Mas de la Brune

A listed historic monument, this beautiful 16thC stone house, with gargoyles and winged creatures on its ornate façade, has views of the old village of Eygalières and a rich history. This is bed-and-breakfast on a very grand scale. Pool.

■ 13810 Eygalières (Bouches-du-Rhône) **Tel** 04 90 95 90 77 **Fax** 04 90 95 99 21 **Meals** breakfast **Prices** FFFF+ **Rooms** 10; all with bath, phone, TV, heating, air-conditioning, hairdryer **Credit cards** MC, V **Closed** 15th Oct-beg-Apr.

Country hotel, Eygalières

Mas dou Pastré

In Van Gogh countryside, this small, converted green-shuttered *mas* has a view of the Alpilles, a swimming-pool, and an owner, Mme Roumanille, who comes from a family of shepherds. With red poppies, white butterflies and exquisitely furnished rooms, it all looks like something out of a magazine.

■ Route d'Organ, 13810 Eygalières (Bouches-du-Rhône) **Tel** 04 90 95 92 61 **Fax** 04 90 95 99 24 **Meals** breakfast; light lunch **Prices** F-FF **Rooms** 11; 8 with bath, 3 with shower; all with phone, TV, heating, minibar, hairdryer **Credit cards** no AE **Closed** never

Coast hotel, Eze

Château Eza

Room service is thrown in for free in this very expensive, very private, hotel – once the home of Prince William of Sweden – perched at the top of the medieval village of Eze. Rooms have terraces with views of the sea way below, or of mountains and are romantically decorated. New American owners. Access by foot.

■ Rue de la Pise, 06360 Eze (Alpes-Maritimes) **Tel** 04 9341 12 24 **Fax** 04 93 41 16 64 **Meals** all **Prices** FFFF+ **Rooms** 7 and 3 suites; all with bath, shower, phone, sat TV, heating, air-conditioning, hairdryer, safe, CD-player, VCR **Credit cards** all **Closed** end Oct-Easter.

Village hotel, Flayosc

La Vieille Bastide

There's a new spirit about the place now that a dynamic, young husband-and-wife team has come from Paris to take over this old *bastide*. Mme d'Aubreby's chic new blue and yellow dining-room is a good omen for the future. Reasonable prices; pool; terrace.

■ 83780 Flayosc (Var) **Tel** 04 94 70 40 57 **Fax** 04 94 84 61 23 **Meals** all **Prices** F-FF **Rooms** 7; all with bath, phone, TV, heating **Credit cards** V **Closed** 1st Oct-30th Mar

Provence-Côte d'Azur

Country inn, Gigondas

Les Florets

An *auberge* since 1870 and set in a refreshingly cool, green, secluded, wooded dell at the foot of the Dentelles de Montmirail, Les Florets is run by a wine-growing family, and serves authentic local fare. Excellent cellar. Good walking country.

■ Route des Dentelles, 84190 Gigondas (Vaucluse) **Tel** 04 90 65 85 01 **Fax** 04 90 65 83 80 **Meals** all **Prices** F-FF **Rooms** 13 double; 8 with bath, 5 with shower; all with phone, heating; some with TV **Credit cards** all **Closed** Jan and Feb

Country hotel, Gordes

Domaine Le Moulin Blanc

This now looks much more like a four-star hotel than a converted mill, but the comfortable Moulin Blanc, run by the helpful Diez family, has a faithful following. Some rooms have small terraces leading out into the garden. Pool. Some road noise.

■ Chemin du Moulin, Les Baumettes, 84220 Gordes (Vaucluse) **Tel** 04 90 72 34 50 **Fax** 04 90 72 25 41 **Meals** all **Prices** FF-FFFF **Rooms** 18; all with bath, phone, TV, minibar (connecting rooms available) **Credit cards** AE, DC, MC, V **Closed** never

Country guest-house, Gordes

La Ferme de la Huppe

'Loved the scale of this dear little group of converted farm buildings' wrote one of our readers. Reception was the cartshed; bedrooms are in the stables. Classical music plays at dinner in the dining-room decorated with farm implements. Pool.

■ Les Porquiers, 84220 Gordes (Vaucluse) **Tel** 04 90 72 12 25 **Fax** 04 90 72 01 83 **Meals** breakfast; dinner (lunch on Sunday only) **Prices** F-FF **Rooms** 8 double; 7 with bath, 1 with shower; all with phone, heating, minibar, sat TV, hairdryer; 4 with air-conditioning **Credit cards** MC, V **Closed** 3rd Nov-end Mar

Country hotel, Gordes

Le Gordos

No restaurant, but few other drawbacks to this *mas de pierre sèche*, just outside Gordes – especially if the Provençal sun shines. Most of the rooms are in outbuildings opening directly on to some part of the garden; there is tennis, as well as an attractive, small pool. 'Very good' service.

■ Route de Cavaillon, 84220 Gordes (Vaucluse) **Tel** 04 90 72 00 75 **Fax** 04 90 72 07 00 **Meals** breakfast, snacks **Prices** F-FFF **Rooms** 19; all with bath or shower, phone, TV **Credit cards** AE, V **Closed** Nov-mid-Mar

Provence-Côte d'Azur

Village hotel, Gordes

Les Romarins

Briskly run by Mme Charles, this is a spotless breakfast-only hotel with a spectacular view from the terrace, and the wide, bay windows, of the terracotta roofs and ochre walls of the pretty – and much visited – village of Gordes. Pool, secure parking.

■ Route de Sénanque, 84220 Gordes (Vaucluse) **Tel** 04 90 72 12 13 **Fax** 04 90 72 13 13 **Meals** breakfast **Prices** FF **Rooms** 10 double; 9 with bath, 1 with shower; all with phone, TV; some with minibar **Credit cards** AE, V **Closed** 15th Jan-15th Feb

Country hotel, Grimaud

La Boulangerie

In a secluded pale pink house – approached up a steep drive – with quiet garden and swimming-pool, this small hotel has country-style furniture, modern paintings and is comfortable, if somewhat cluttered. Mme Piget is most welcoming.

■ Route de Collobrières, 83310 Grimaud (Var) **Tel** 04 94 43 23 16 **Fax** 04 94 43 38 27 **Meals** breakfast, lunch **Prices** FF-FFFF **Rooms** 11 double; with bath, phone, heating, TV **Credit cards** all except DC **Closed** 15th Oct-Easter

Country hotel, Ile de la Barthelasse

La Ferme

This pale yellow, green-shuttered hotel on the verdant island of fruit orchards across the river from Avignon is recommended for its dependable, bargain-priced cuisine. The sound of crickets here, instead of the sound of traffic.

■ Chemin des Bois, Ile de la Barthelasse, 84000 Avignon **Tel** 04 90 82 57 53 **Fax** 04 90 27 15 47 **Meals** all **Prices** F-FF **Rooms** 20; 10 with bath, 10 with shower; all with phone, TV, heating; 10 with air-conditioning **Credit cards** all major **Closed** 4th Nov-end Feb

Seaside hotel, Ile de Port-Cros

Le Manoir

This large green-shuttered 19thC manor house stands on a lush, secluded island (a nature reserve) a few km off the south coast and is run along house-party lines. White-walled bedrooms are furnished with 19thC pieces – simple, but stylish and comfortable. Good seafood.

■ Ile de Port-Cros, 83400 Hyères (Var) **Tel** 04 94 05 90 52 **Fax** 04 94 05 90 89 **Meals** all **Prices** FF-FFFF **Rooms** 23; all with bath or shower, central heating, phone **Credit cards** MC, V **Closed** Oct-Apr

Provence-Côte d'Azur

Country hotel, Isle-sur-la-Sorgue

Mas de Cure Bourse

La patronne, Françoise Donzé, one of France's most talented women cooks, can be seen busily at work in her kitchen preparing her grandmother's recipes, with her famous artichoke in her chef's *toque*. Rooms are comfortable, but the food is clearly the attraction of the hotel, once an 18thC *relais de poste*. Pool.

■ Route de Caumont-sur-Durance, 84800 Isle-sur-la-Sorgue (Vaucluse) **Tel** 04 90 38 16 58 **Fax** 04 90 38 52 31 **Meals** all **Prices** F-FF **Rooms** 13; with bath, phone, TV **Credit cards** MC, V **Closed** never

Country hotel, Lagnes

Mas des Grès

The Crovaras, an enthusiastic young Swiss couple, have taken over this green-shuttered, pale-pink hotel, with gravelled terrace under plane trees, where dinner is served on little metal tables. Thierry Crovara is an excellent cook. Pool.

■ La Route d'Apt, 84800 Lagnes (Vaucluse) **Tel** 04 90 20 32 85 **Fax** 04 90 20 21 45 **Meals** breakfast; dinner **Prices** FF **Rooms** 14; all with bath and heating; some with TV; hairdryer on request **Credit cards** MC, V **Closed** Dec-Mar

Seaside hotel, Le Lavandou

Auberge de la Calanque

This arcaded hotel overlooking the marina of Le Lavandou comes strongly recommended by a reader, despite its size – not only for the 'fantastic' view but also the 'very comfortable, airy' rooms and 'very helpful' manager. Restaurant in the hotel, and plenty of others nearby.

■ 62 Avenue du Général de Gaulle, 83980 Le Lavandou (Var) **Tel** 04 94 71 05 96 **Fax** 04 94 71 20 12 **Meals** all **Prices** FF-FFFF **Rooms** 38; all with bath/shower, central heating, phone, TV **Credit cards** AE, DC, MC, V **Closed** Nov-mid-Mar

Village hotel, Lourmarin

Le Moulin de Lourmarin

In a popular Luberon village, this pale yellow stone building used to be the olive mill and has been smartly restored with modern art and Provençal print fabrics. Top-floor rooms have terraces with views. Chef Edouard Loubet has a Michelin star.

■ 4, rue de Temple, 84160 Lourmarin (Vaucluse) **Tel** 04 90 68 06 69 **Fax** 04 90 68 31 76 **Meals** all **Prices** FFF-FFFF **Rooms** 17 and 3 apartments; all with bath or shower, phone, TV, air-conditioning **Credit cards** AE, DC, MC, V **Closed** 15th Jan-16th Feb

Provence-Côte d'Azur

Château guest-house, Malemort-du-Comtat

Château Unang

Marie-Hélène Lefer – whose brother runs the family vineyard nearby – receives guests at this elegant, restful, creeper-clad house. Bedrooms have marble fireplaces. Mozart plays as Château Unang red, white and rosé is served at dinner on the terrace.

■ Route de Méthamis, 84570 Malemort-du-Comtat (Vaucluse) **Tel** 04 90 69 71 06 **Fax** 04 90 69 92 80 **Meals** breakfast; dinner **Prices** FF **Rooms** 4 double; all with bath **Credit cards** MC, V **Closed** never

Village hotel, Maussane-les-Alpilles

l'Oustaloun

Filled with charm and character, this little hotel puts its tables out under the plane trees in the square of a delightful Alpilles village in the summer or uses its 16thC vaulted dining-room. Bedrooms are simple (some may be noisy); kitchen uses fresh produce for local and Italian specialities.

■ Place de l'Église, 13520 Maussanne-les-Alpilles (Bouches-du-Rhône) **Tel** 04 90 54 32 19 **Fax** 04 90 54 45 58 **Meals** all **Prices** F **Rooms** 10; most with shower, 4 with bath; 8 with TV **Credit cards** AE, MC, V **Closed** 8th Jan-15th Feb

Restaurant with rooms, Mondragon

La Beaugravière

A specialist in truffles, Guy Jullien cooks memorable meals, served on a shady terrace in summer or in the dining-room decorated with illustrations of vine species. Modest, clean rooms upstairs are double-glazed to keep out road noise.

■ RN7, 84430 Mondragon (Vaucluse) **Tel** 04 90 40 82 54 **Fax** 04 90 40 91 01 **Meals** all **Prices** F **Rooms** 3; none with bath; all with phone, heating **Credit cards** MC, V **Closed** 15th-30th Sept

Suburban villa, Montfavet

Les Frênes

The four-star Relais & Châteaux family-run Les Frênes looks like an iced cake, with pale-pink walls and pale-green shutters. Set in a neat park, its rooms are luxuriously furnished and chef Antoine Biaconi's tempting dishes are served on Limoges china. Swimming-pool.

■ Avenue Vertes Rives, 84140 Montfavet-Avignon (Vaucluse) **Tel** 04 90 31 17 93 **Fax** 04 90 23 95 04 **Meals** all **Prices** FFF-FFFF+ **Rooms** 20; all with bath, phone, sat TV, heating, air-conditioning, minibar, hairdryer, safe **Credit cards** all **Closed** 15th Nov-15th Mar

Provence-Côte d'Azur

Village hotel, Montferrat

La Calanco

Large rooms, informal ambience and home-cooking in a handsome 400-year-old house in centre of unspoiled village. Owner Katrin Kuhlmann is gathering quite a following with her considerate and unobtrusive ways.

■ 20, rue du Docteur Rayol, 83131 Montferrat (Var) **Tel** 04 94 70 93 10 **Fax** 04 94 70 91 49 **Meals** breakfast and dinner **Prices** F **Rooms** 4; 2 with bath, 2 with shower; all with heating **Credit cards** V **Closed** never

Country manor house, Mougins

Manoir de l'Etang

This expensive, comfortable, and extremely pretty, vine-clad, white-shuttered hotel has a large, beautiful garden – and a lily-filled pond. It is a quiet, orderly, elegant retreat from the bustle of fashionable Mougins. Pool; terrace.

■ Les Bois de Font-Merle, 06250 Mougins (Alpes-Maritimes) **Tel** 04 93 90 01 07 **Fax** 04 92 92 20 70 **Meals** all **Prices** FF-FFFF **Rooms** 15 and 2 apartments; most with bath; all with phone, TV, heating, fan, minibar; some with hairdryer **Credit cards** no DC **Closed** 1st Nov-mid-Dec; all Feb

Country hotel, Moustiers-Ste-Marie

Auberge de la Ferme Rose

Basic bedrooms are on the top floor of this small isolated hotel at the end of a rough track outside the pretty village of Moustiers. Downstairs reflects the owner's retro taste: a '50s juke-box, the bar from the old Brasserie Noailles in Marseille.

■ 04360 Moustiers-Ste-Marie (Alpes-de-Haute-Provence) **Tel** 04 92 74 69 47 **Fax** 04 92 74 60 76 **Meals** breakfast only **Prices** F **Rooms** 6 doubles with showers, phone, heating **Credit cards** all **Closed** never

Country house hotel, Nans-les-Pins

Domaine de Châteauneuf

A luxuriously comfortable four-star Relais & Châteaux with an 18-hole golf course, three tennis courts, and a pool in the grounds – and ducks. Hard to imagine that Napoléon slept here.

■ 83860 Nans-les-Pins (Var) **Tel** 04 94 78 90 06 **Fax** 04 94 78 63 30 **Meals** all **Prices** FF-FFFF **Rooms** 30l 24 with bath, 6 with shower; all with phone, sat TV, minibar **Credit cards** AE, DC, MC, V **Closed** Dec-Feb

Provence-Côte d'Azur

Manor house hotel, Noves

Auberge de Noves

The charm here is that of owner M Lalleman, who takes a close, personal interest in his guests (try his delicious well water at meals). His son, Robert, is chef; the kitchens have a Michelin star. Rooms are wildly expensive, but readers tell us they are worth every penny. Pool; terrace; four-star comfort. Helipad.

■ 13550 Noves (Bouches-du-Rhône) **Tel** 04 90 94 19 21 **Fax** 04 90 94 47 76 **Meals** all **Prices** FFFF+ **Rooms** 20; all with bath, phone, TV, air-conditioning, minibar **Credit cards** AE, DC, V **Closed** Jan

Country hotel, Oppède

Mas des Capelans

A restored 18thC silk-breeders' residence, set among vineyards, this is a relaxed and welcoming place, where the Poiri family give complimentary cocktails and serve dinner under mulberry trees. Beamed sitting-room; country bedrooms; heated pool.

■ 84580 Oppède (Vaucluse) **Tel** 04 90 76 99 04 **Fax** 04 90 76 90 29 **Meals** breakfast; dinner **Prices** FF-FFFF **Rooms** 9; 8 with bath, 1 with shower; all with phone, TV, heating, hairdryer; 3 with terrace **Credit cards** AE, V **Closed** 14th Nov-15th Feb

Country hotel, Pégomas

Le Bosquet

This modern hotel with a spacious garden but no restaurant has a special place in the affections of many British and other foreign visitors – probably due to the relaxed atmosphere, coupled with the very un-Provençal prices. Pool, tennis. Our most recent reporter was very happy here.

■ Quartier du Château, 06580 Pégomas (Alpes-Maritimes) **Tel** 04 93 42 22 87 **Meals** breakfast only **Prices** F-FF **Rooms** 24; all with bath or shower, central heating, phone **Credit cards** not accepted **Closed** 1st Nov

Country guest-house, Plan-de-la-Tour

Mas de Brugassières

'An excellent place to unwind after the long drive south,' is the verdict of one visitor to this modern (1974) 'farmhouse', set in lush gardens surrounded by vineyards. Some bedrooms open directly on to the garden and swimming-pool. Parking.

■ Plan-de-la-Tour, 83120 Ste-Maxime (Var) **Tel** 04 94 43 72 42 **Fax** 04 94 43 00 20 **Meals** breakfast only; light lunch in season **Prices** FF **Rooms** 14 double; all with bath and shower; central heating, phone **Credit cards** MC, V **Closed** Nov-mid-Mar

Provence-Côte d'Azur

Seaside hotel, Ramatuelle

La Ferme d'Augustin

In a large garden, 100 metres from Tahiti Beach and five minutes from the centre of St-Tropez, this is a relaxed, friendly hotel, filled with old country furniture. Bedrooms are in various buildings; terraces; heated pool with hydro-massage.

■ Plage de Tahiti, 83350 Ramatuelle (Var) **Tel** 04 94 97 23 83 **Fax** 04 94 97 40 30 **Meals** breakfast only **Prices** FF-FFFF **Rooms** 46; most with bath; all with phone, minibar, hairdryer, safe; some with air-conditioning; TV on request **Credit cards** all except DC **Closed** 20th Oct-end Mar

Village hotel, Roquebrune-Village

Hôtel les Deux Frères

This immediately appealing, Dutch-owned hotel is named after two rocks and is decorated throughout in simple, good taste, with much modern art. Staff are young and informal. Restaurant is Michelin-starred; show-business people eat here.

■ 06190 Roquebrune-Village, Cap-Martin (Alpes-Maritimes) **Tel** 04 93 28 99 00 **Fax** 04 93 28 99 10 **Meals** all **Prices** FF **Rooms** 10; 8 double; all have bath, phone, TV, heating **Credit cards** all except DC **Closed** 15th Nov-15th Dec

Country hotel, Roquefort-les-Pins

Auberge du Colombier

An old *mas*, long and white, set among tall, shady trees, with views over wooded hills to the sea, this attractive *auberge* has a terrace for summer eating, a swimming-pool and a tennis court. Rooms are relatively functional and plain; the garden is lush.

■ 06330 Roquefort-les-Pins (Alpes-Maritimes) **Tel** 04 93 77 10 27 **Fax** 04 93 77 07 03 **Meals** all **Prices** F-FFF **Rooms** 18 double, 2 apartments; all with bath, phone, TV **Credit cards** AE, DC, MC, V **Closed** Jan

Village hotel, Saignon

Auberge du Presbytère

In three village houses, with delightfully uneven floor levels, the Bernardi family provide simple, but pretty, rooms with period furniture and Provençal fabrics. Lunch in the village square by the fountain. Excellent value; copious cuisine.

■ Place de la Fontaine, 84400 Saignon (Vaucluse) **Tel** 04 90 74 11 50 **Fax** 04 90 04 68 51 **Meals** all **Prices** F **Rooms** 8; 6 with bath, 2 with shower; all with heating **Credit cards** all **Closed** 15th-30th Nov; all Jan

Provence-Côte d'Azur

Restaurant with rooms, St-Andiol

Le Berger des Abeilles

Nicole Grenier, a celebrated cook, was born in this shuttered farmhouse that now caters for her large circle of admirers. Rooms upstairs are ordinary, but clean; all the action is downstairs in the beamed dining-room or out on the shaded terrace. Mme Grenier puts her heart into her *cuisine provençale.*

■ RD 74E, 13670 St-Andiol (Bouches-du-Rhône) **Tel** 04 90 95 01 91 **Fax** 04 90 95 48 26 **Meals** all **Prices** F **Rooms** 6; 3 with bath, 3 with shower; all with phone, TV, heating **Credit cards** all except DC **Closed** Jan and Feb

Seaside hotel, St-Clair

Hôtel Belle-Vue

This informal seaside hotel in lush, colourful gardens lives up to its name, with a wonderful view across the bay. It offers unpretentious but comfortable accommodation: bedrooms vary – the best are bright and spacious, with big new bathrooms; some have sea views. More reports welcome.

■ Blvd du Four des Maures, St-Clair, 83980 Le Lavandou (Var) **Tel** 04 94 71 01 06 **Fax** 04 94 71 64 72 **Meals** all **Prices** F-FFF **Rooms** 19; all with bath or shower, central heating, phone **Credit cards** AE, DC, MC, V **Closed** Nov-Mar.

Villa guest-house, St-Jean-Cap-Ferrat

Clair Logis

It is not easy to find a reasonably priced hotel in such an exclusive area, let alone one which has the charm of a private villa and is set in lush, secluded gardens. Bedrooms are simple (those in the annexe are not particularly spacious) and four can accommodate families. No restaurant.

■ 12 Avenue Centrale, 06230 St-Jean-Cap-Ferrat (Alpes-Maritimes) **Tel** 0493 76 04 57 **Fax** 04 93 76 11 85 **Meals** breakfast only **Prices** F-FF **Rooms** 18; all with bath, central heating, phone; most have TV, minibar **Credit cards** AE, DC, MC, V **Closed** mid-Nov-mid-Dec

Camargue hotel, Les Stes-Maries-de-la-Mer

Mas de Clarousset

This little white hotel has a row of comfortable, attractive rooms looking out over the marshes (and flamingos) and a long, covered terrace by the pool. Mme Henriette takes everyone under her wing and makes them feel at home.

■ La Roubine de Joly, 13460 Les Stes-Maries-de-la-Mer (Bouches-du-Rhône) **Tel** 04 90 97 81 66 **Fax** 04 90 97 88 59 **Meals** all **Prices** FFF **Rooms** 10; all with bath, shower, phone, sat TV, heating, minibar, individual garage **Credit cards** all **Closed** never

Provence-Côte d'Azur

Village hotel, St-Paul-de-Vence

La Colombe d'Or

A famous, chic small hotel, distinguished by a collection of modern art, but also a delightful place to stay. All is simple and in exquisite 'country' taste; outside there is a creeper-surrounded terrace. The food wins no awards, but that hardly matters.

■ Place de Gaulle, 06570 St-Paul-de-Vence (Alpes-Maritimes) **Tel** 04 93 32 80 02 **Fax** 04 93 32 77 88 **Meals** all **Prices** FFFF **Rooms** 25; all with bath, some with spa baths, central heating, air-conditioning, phone, TV **Credit cards** AE, DC, MC, V **Closed** mid-Nov-mid-Dec

Country villa, St-Paul-de-Vence

Les Orangers

A traditional Provençal house in a fine hillside setting (views), furnished with simple good taste and immaculately kept. In the sitting-room there are exposed beams, solid antiques, fresh flowers; most of the bedrooms have balconies or terraces. 'A lovely hotel despite the busy street,' enthuses a visitor.

■ Chemin des Fumerates, 06570 St-Paul-de-Vence (Alpes-Maritimes) **Tel** 04 93 32 80 95 **Fax** 04 93 32 00 32 **Meals** breakfast **Prices** FF-FFF **Rooms** 10; all with bath, heating, phone **Credit cards** MC, V **Closed** never

Village hotel, St-Paul-de-Vence

Le Saint-Paul

If you can afford it, here is another exceptionally captivating place to stay in pricey St-Paul, in a beautifully restored 16thC house. Bedrooms are done out with real panache, and the public areas are equally welcoming; there is a small dining terrace. Above-average cooking.

■ 86 Grande Rue, 06570 St-Paul-de-Vence (Alpes-Maritimes) **Tel** 04 93 32 65 25 **Fax** 04 93 32 52 94 **Meals** all **Prices** FFF-FFFF **Rooms** 18; all with bath, air-conditioning, sat TV, minibar, safe **Credit cards** AE, DC, MC, V **Closed** 8th Jan-16th Feb

Town hotel, St-Rémy-de-Provence

Hôtel des Arts

The shady pavement tables of this unpretentious place have long been a happy spot to sit and watch the Provençal world go by. The restaurant serves well-cooked, reasonably priced, simple food (liberally laced with the region's herbs). Bedrooms seem secondary, but are done out in rustic style.

■ 30 Blvd Victor-Hugo, 13210 St-Rémy-de-Provence (Bouches-du-Rhône) **Tel** 04 90 92 08 50 **Fax** 04 90 92 55 09 **Meals** all **Prices** F **Rooms** 17; all with central heating, phone **Credit cards** AE, MC, V **Closed** Feb

Provence-Côte d'Azur

Château hotel, St-Rémy-de-Provence

Château des Alpilles

An elegant, upright 19thC manor house offering an atmosphere of gracious living combined with the facilities of a modern luxury hotel. Bedrooms are spacious and furnished with antiques, the bathrooms marble and modern. Food is served by the swimming-pool in summer.

■ RD 31, 13210 St-Rémy-de-Provence (Bouches-du-Rhône) **Tel** 04 90 92 03 33 **Fax** 04 90 92 45 17 **Meals** breakfast **Prices** FFFF **Rooms** 20; all with bath, central heating, phone, sat TV, minibar **Credit cards** AE, DC, MC, V **Closed** Jan to Mar

Country hotel, St-Rémy-de-Provence

Domaine de Valmouriane

Once the property of French racing driver Olivier Gendebien, this hotel is furnished in a mixture of styles and has a relaxed and welcoming atmosphere. The Alpilles are within touching distance. There's a strange pool that takes some getting used to.

■ 13210 St-Rémy-de-Provence (Bouches-du-Rhône) **Tel** 04 90 92 44 62 **Fax** 04 90 92 37 32 **Meals** all **Prices** FF-FFFF **Rooms** 14; all with bath, phone, sat TV, heating, minibar, hairdryer **Credit cards** AE, DC, MC, V **Closed** never

Country guest-house, Saturnin-les-Apt

La Maison Garance

A Parisian photographer, Pascal Bennet, and his wife, Marie-Christine, let rooms in their stylishly-decorated house, and serve breakfast under the fig tree in the courtyard – also a light lunch, with Luberon wines, in the garden by the pool.

■ Hameau des Bassacs, 84490 St-Saturnin-les-Apt (Vaucluse) **Tel** 04 90 05 74 61 **Fax** 04 90 05 75 68 **Meals** breakfast; lunch **Prices** FF **Rooms** 5 double; all with bath, phone, heating **Credit cards** V **Closed** 15th Nov-15th Dec

Seaside villa, St-Tropez

Le Yaca

This smart little hotel has been cleverly converted from three 200-year-old buildings, using a confusing mix of styles, but with 'rustic chic' predominating. Bedrooms are furnished with antiques, simply decorated in a typical southern style, but with all the comforts.

■ 1 Blvd d'Aumale, 83990 St-Tropez (Var) **Tel** 04 94 97 11 79 **Fax** 04 94 97 58 50 **Meals** breakfast **Prices** FFFF **Rooms** 23; all with bath, central heating, air-conditioning, phone, TV, minibar **Credit cards** AE, DC, MC, V **Closed** mid-Oct-Easter

Provence-Côte d'Azur

Converted abbey, Salon-de-Provence

Abbaye de Sainte Croix

Saved from ruin in 1969 and turned into a luxury, four-star Relais & Châteaux, this 12thC abbey on a hill has a warren of stone passages and splendid views of the valley below. The vaulted dining-room was the chapel; a mass was celebrated there in 1993 to mark a century of interruption. Pool.

■ Val de Cuech, 13300 Salon-de-Provence (Bouches-du-Rhône) **Tel** 04 90 56 24 55 **Fax** 04 90 56 31 12 **Meals** all **Prices** FFF-FFFF **Credit cards** all **Closed** 3rd Nov-mid-Mar

Seaside hotel, Sanary

Le Castel

Unassuming, reassuringly old-fashioned small hotel (Logis) much nearer to Bandol than to Sanary – and spotlessly clean. M Palacios (Spanish, chef and something of an artist) built this low house 12 years ago as a restaurant. Rooms, added later, all have terraces where breakfast is served. Modest prices.

■ 925 Route de la Canolle, 83110 Sanary-sur-Mer (Var) **Tel** 04 94 29 82 98 **Fax** 04 94 32 53 32 **Meals** all **Prices** F **Rooms** 9; 3 with bath, all with shower; all with phone, TV, heating **Credit cards** all **Closed** 2 weeks in winter

Village hotel, Séguret

La Table du Comtat

Built against the hillside above a tiny, unspoiled medieval village, this hotel enjoys wonderful views. The much-modernized interior is light, airy and spacious, with attractive fabrics and furniture. Excellent, eclectic food. Michelin-starred.

■ Séguret, 84110 Vaison-la-Romaine (Vaucluse) **Tel** 04 90 46 91 49 **Fax** 04 90 46 94 27 **Meals** all **Prices** FF **Rooms** 8; all with bath, heating, phone, TV **Credit cards** AE, DC, MC, V **Closed** Tues and Wed, except July, August, Easter and Christmas

Country hotel, Sérignan-du-Comtat

Hostellerie du Vieux Château

In a picturesque village in the middle of a great plain of Côtes du Rhône vineyards, this handsome old 18thC farmhouse is now a Logis with modest bedrooms – one has pictures of geese in it – and gastronomic menus prepared by *patron* M Truchot. Pool.

■ Route de Ste-Cecile-les-Vignes, 84830 Sérignan-du-Comtat (Vaucluse) **Tel** 04 90 70 05 5 **Fax** 04 90 70 05 62 **Meals** all **Prices** F-FFF **Rooms** 7; 6 with bath, 1 with shower; all with phone, TV, heating, minibar, hairdryer **Credit cards** AE, MC **Closed** 1 week in Nov; 1 week at Christmas

Provence-Côte d'Azur

Country hotel, Tourtour

La Bastide de Tourtour

This modern but traditional-style hotel offers comfort and attentive service (it is in the Relais & Châteaux group), and the food is excellent, if not in the first rank. For many, the key attraction is the secluded setting, high up among pine forests. Swimming-pool.

■ Route de Draguignan, Tourtour, 83690 Salernes (Var) **Tel** 04 94 70 57 30 **Fax** 04 94 70 54 90 **Meals** all **Prices** FF-FFFF **Rooms** 25; all with bath, central heating, phone, TV, minibar **Credit cards** AE, DC, V **Closed** Nov-mid-Mar

Village hotel, Vénasque

Auberge de la Fontaine

This pretty little 18thC hotel, in a village classed as one of the most beautiful in France, provides cleverly-designed and comfortable suites of rooms, with kitchens, giving total privacy and independence. Downstairs is a bistro.

■ Place de la Fontaine, 84210 Vénasque (Vaucluse) **Tel** 04 90 66 02 96 **Fax** 04 90 66 13 14 **Meals** all **Prices** FF-FFF **Rooms** 5; all with bath, phone, TV, heating, minibar, washing-up machine, fridge, open fireplace (wood provided); 4 with air-conditioning; 4 with terrace **Credit cards** MC, V **Closed** never

Town inn, Vence

Auberge des Seigneurs et du Lion d'Or

Our reporter felt nothing much had changed here in the last 50 years and therein lies the charm. Bedrooms are named after frequent visitors – Dufy, Bonnard, Soutine, Modigliani, Chagall – and are fairly Spartan. The dining-room has olive wood tables, and copper pans hanging over the fireplace. Traditional food.

■ Place du Frêne, 06140 Vence (Alpes-Maritimes) **Tel** 04 93 58 04 24 **Fax** 04 93 24 08 01 **Meals** all **Prices** F **Rooms** 6; all with shower, heating; hairdryer on request **Credit cards** all **Closed** 15th Nov-15th Mar

Town villa, Villefranche-sur-Mer

Hôtel la Flore

Not in the pretty old part of Villefranche, but with spectacular sea views, this pleasant *fin-de-siècle* villa has a proud, friendly owner and rooms with terraces. Bedrooms are fresh and white; bathrooms are sparkling. Pool; fresh flowers.

■ Blvd Princesse Grace de Monaco, 06230 Villefranche-sur-Mer (Alpes-Maritimes) **Tel** 04 93 76 30 30 **Fax** 04 93 76 99 99 **Meals** all **Prices** F-FFF **Rooms** 23 double; with bath or shower; all with phone, sat TV, heating, air-conditioning, minibar, hairdryer, safe **Credit cards** all **Closed** never

The Rhône Valley

Country hotel, Baix

La Cardinale et Sa Résidence

The birthplace of the Relais & Châteaux chain, La Cardinale is a welcoming old house, with four beautiful bedrooms; the rest, along with a smart swimming-pool, are 3 km away at the Résidence.

■ Quai du Rhône, 07210 Baix (Ardèche) **Tel** 04 75 85 80 40 **Fax** 04 75 85 82 07 **Meals** all **Prices** FFF-FFFF **Rooms** 14; all with bath or shower, phone, TV, air-conditioning, heating, minibar **Credit cards** AE, DC, MC, V **Closed** 1st Feb-10th Mar

Farmhouse hotel, Chonas-l'Amballan

Le Marais Saint-Jean

Owned by the Girardons of nearby Domaine de Clairefontaine, this neat farmhouse conversion has all modern comforts and original timbered ceilings, beams and floor tiles. Excellent Girardon food is served in the beamed dining-room or on the terrace.

■ 38121 Chonas-l'Amballan (Isère) **Tel** 04 74 58 83 28 **Fax** 04 74 58 81 96 **Meals** all **Prices** FF **Rooms** 10; all with bath, phone, sat TV, heating, air-conditioning, minibar, hairdryer **Credit cards** AE, DC, MC, V **Closed** Feb

Village inn, Cliousclat

La Treille Muscate

This charming, ivy-covered inn, in a small perched village, has sunny, ochre walls, stencilling, tiled floors, dried flowers, wrought-iron furnishings and cheerful Provençal fabrics. The terrace and many bedrooms have expansive views of the Rhône valley. Pity about the nuclear plant in the distance.

■ 26270 Cliousclat (Drôme) **Tel** 04 75 63 13 10 **Fax** 04 75 63 10 79 **Meals** all **Prices** F-FF **Rooms** 12; all with bath or shower, phone, heating; TV and hairdryers on request **Credit cards** MC, V **Closed** Jan-Feb

Riverside hotel, Condrieu

Hôtellerie Beau Rivage

With Condrieu's famous vineyards on the hill behind and the Rhône on the front doorstep, this Relais & Châteaux has a most pleasing position – and a Michelin star. Comfortable bedrooms are sometimes a little over-decorated and fussy, but the riverside terrace is charming.

■ 69420 Condrieu (Rhône) **Tel** 04 74 59 52 24 **Fax** 04 74 59 59 36 **Meals** all **Prices** FF-FFFF **Rooms** 25, all with bath, phone, sat TV, heating, minibar; many with air-conditioning **Credit cards** AE, MC, V **Closed** never

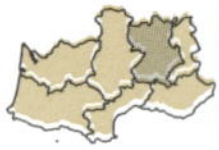

The Rhône Valley

Manor house hotel, Grignan

Manoir de la Roseraie

This private manor house was built by the Mayor of Grignan in 1853 and has more than 350 rose bushes in the large garden, which is also planted with cedars. Bedrooms are stylishly decorated and one has a circular bath. There's a heated swimming-pool.

■ Route de Valréas, 26230 Grignan (Drôme) **Tel** 04 75 46 58 15 **Fax** 04 75 46 91 55 **Meals** all **Prices** FFF-FFFF **Rooms** 15; all with bath, phone, sat TV, heating **Credit cards** AE, DC, MC, V **Closed** 6th Jan-15th Feb

Château hotel, Lamastre

Château d'Urbilhac

This fairy-tale château – 19thC but in Renaissance style, with round tower and a steep roof – has a peaceful, elevated setting in a large park, with a pleasant pool. The interior is rather ponderous, but does not lack character or comfort. 'Good food,' but 'atmosphere a little stilted' comments a visitor.

■ 07270 Lamastre (Ardèche) **Tel** 04 75 06 52 75 **Meals** all **Prices** F-FF (*demi-pension* obligatory in season) **Rooms** 13; all with bath or shower, phone **Credit cards** AE, DC, MC, V **Closed** Oct-Apr.

Town hotel, Lamastre

Hôtel du Midi

The restaurant is the heart of this hotel, serving a very successful blend of traditional and *nouvelle* dishes. The dining-rooms are rather plain, but intimate; service is helpful and friendly. Bedrooms, in a separate building a minute's walk away, are comfortably spacious and tastefully furnished.

■ Place Seignobos, 07270 Lamastre (Ardèche) **Tel** 04 75 06 41 50 **Fax** 04 75 06 49 75 **Meals** all **Prices** F-FF **Rooms** 13; all with bath or shower, central heating, phone; some with TV **Credit cards** AE, DC, MC, V **Closed** mid-Dec-Feb; Sun evening, Mon

Village hotel, Mirmande

La Capitelle

A rough stone building in a backwater setting in a walled medieval village, yet only a few minutes' drive from the *autoroute*, La Capitelle makes an excellent stopover. It has an air of confident good taste, with a stylishly traditional feel to the individually and boldly decorated bedrooms, and the vaulted dining-room.

■ Le Rempart, 26270 Mirmande (Drôme) **Tel** 04 75 63 02 72 **Fax** 04 75 63 02 50 **Meals** all **Prices** F-FF **Rooms** 11, all with bath or shower, central heating, phone **Credit cards** AE, DC, MC, V **Closed** mid-Jan-mid-Feb; Tue and Wed lunch

The Rhône Valley

Medieval inn, Pérouges

Hostellerie du Vieux Pérouges

In a perfectly preserved little medieval town, this timbered inn serves up local fare in a charming old-style restaurant. Spacious bedrooms in the two 14thC buildings are a copy of medieval sleeping quarters, right down to canopied beds. Simpler rooms in the 18thC annexe are less expensive. One of the oldest inns in France.

■ Place du Tilleul, 01800 Pérouges (Ain) **Tel** 04 74 61 00 88 **Fax** 04 74 34 77 90 **Meals** all **Prices** FF-FFFF **Rooms** 28; all with bath, phone, TV, heating; some with hairdryers **Credit cards** MC, V **Closed** never

Château hotel, Rochegude

Château de Rochegude

Despite the high cost of rooms here, we cannot resist including this sumptuous château because of its wonderful setting – overlooking the vineyards of the Rhône plain – and its equally wonderful food. Bedrooms are palatial. Relais & Châteaux.

■ 26790 Rochegude (Drôme) **Tel** 04 75 97 21 10 **Fax** 04 75 04 89 87 **Meals** all **Prices** FFF-FFFF **Rooms** 26 double, 4 suites; all with bath, phone, sat TV, heating, air-conditioning, minibar **Credit cards** AE, DC, MC, V **Closed** mid-Jan-mid-Mar

Country hotel, La Rochette-sur-Crest

Auberge de la Rochette

At the foot of the Vercors, among fields of garlic, this attractively decorated, green-shuttered old farmhouse has pretty Provençal prints in the bedrooms and in the dining-room. Food is excellent; service friendly and informal. Pool, private parking.

■ La Rochette-sur-Crest, 26400 Vauvaneys-la-Rochette (Drôme) **Tel** 04 75 25 79 30 **Fax** 04 75 25 79 25 **Meals** all **Prices** FF **Rooms** 5; all with bath or shower, phone, TV, minibar, safe **Credit cards** MC, V **Closed** 2 weeks Oct, 2 weeks Feb

Farm guest-house, St-Cierge-la-Serre

Grangeon

There's no TV and no phone in the rooms in this remote place, 4 km from the nearest village and reached by a winding road through hills and woods. Mme Valetta bakes her own bread and cooks with fresh vegetables from her *potager*. Strictly for escapists.

■ 07800 St-Cierge-la-Serre (Ardèche) **Tel** 04 76 65 73 86 **Fax** none **Meals** breakfast, dinner **Prices** F-FF **Rooms** 5; 4 with bath, 1 with shower; all with central heating; two rooms share WC **Credit cards** none **Closed** Nov-Easter

The Rhône Valley

Country inn, St-Lattier

Le Lièvre Amoureux

This old *auberge de chasse*, set among corn fields and with a gabled overhung roof, has excellent food, a terrace, and a pool which is directly accessible from the pine-panelled rooms in the modern annexe. The older buildings have more traditional (and less expensive) rooms, which we prefer.

■ 38840 St-Lattier (Isère) **Tel** 04 76 64 50 67 **Fax** 04 76 64 31 21 **Meals** all **Prices** F-FF **Rooms** 12; all with bath, phone, heating; those in annexe have TV, hairdryer **Credit cards** AE, DC, MC, V **Closed** mid-Oct-end Mar

Village inn, St-Restitut

Auberge des Quatre Saisons

The vine-clad *auberge* is a conversion of two Romanesque houses on the square of a medieval perched village that one of our readers says is so sleepy as to be comatose. Bedrooms are quiet, rather dark and cosy. Regional fare served in the restaurant.

■ Place de l'Église, 26130 St-Restitut (Drôme) **Tel** 04 75 04 71 88 **Fax** 04 75 04 70 88 **Meals** all **Prices** F-FF **Rooms** 10; all with bath or shower, phone; 5 with TV **Credit cards** all major **Closed** Jan

Château hotel, St-Sauveur-en-Rue

Auberge du Château de Bobigneux

There's a working farm attached to this small, bargain-priced hotel in wine country: the family room overlooks the farmyard in order to amuse the children. Owners, the Labères, keep a relaxed, friendly house and provide meals using produce from the garden.

■ 42200 St-Sauveur-en-Rue (Loire) **Tel** 04 77 39 24 33 **Fax** 04 77 39 25 74 **Meals** all **Prices** F **Rooms** 6 double and 1 family room; most with shower **Credit cards** all **Closed** Jan and Feb

Country hotel, Solerieux

La Ferme Saint-Michel

This beautiful stone farmhouse, dating from the 16thC, is surrounded by fields of lavender and vineyards and is close to the château of the famous Mme de Sévigné. Very attractive, very comfortable, excellent value. Terrace, pool, private parking.

■ Route D341, 26130 Solerieux (Drôme) **Tel** 04 75 98 10 66 **Fax** 04 75 98 19 09 **Meals** all **Prices** F **Rooms** 14; all with bath, phone, TV, heating, hairdryer; some with air-conditioning; 1 room with WC in hall **Credit cards** MC, V **Closed** never

The Rhône Valley/The Alps

Village inn, Vallon-Pont-d'Arc

Manoir du Raveyron

This is the sort of rustic village inn that is the bedrock of French hotel keeping – a two-fireplace Logis offering simple but satisfactory accommodation, modest prices, a warm welcome and excellent, wholesome food. In gated courtyard.

■ Rue Henri Barbusse, 07150 Vallon-Pont-d'Arc (Ardèche) **Tel** 04 75 88 03 59 **Fax** 04 75 37 11 12 **Meals** all **Prices** F **Rooms** 15 double, 1 single; all with shower, central heating. **Credit cards** MC, V **Closed** mid-Oct-mid-Mar

Converted abbey, Annecy-le-Vieux (The Alps)

L'Abbaye

In an unsightly sprawling residential part of Annecy, this is a surprisingly attractive hotel with cobbled courtyard, wooden balcony and exotically-decorated vaulted dining-room. Four-star comfort. (Disco in separate building.) Delightful garden.

■ 15, Chemin de l'Abbaye, 74940 Annecy-le-Vieux (Haute-Savoie) **Tel** 04 50 23 61 08 **Fax** 04 50 27 77 65 **Meals** breakfast; dinner **Prices** FF **Rooms** 15 double; all with bath, heating, phone, TV, minibar **Credit cards** all major **Closed** restaurant only, Mon

Country hotel, Chamonix (The Alps)

Chalet-Hôtel Beausoleil

At the foot of the Aiguille du Midi and Mont Blanc, this peaceful, family-run hotel, with delightful garden, is surrounded by fields. Rooms are recently-renovated; recommended for family cooking.

■ Le Lavancher, 74400 Chamonix (Haute-Savoie) **Tel** 04 50 54 00 78 **Fax** 04 50 54 17 34 **Meals** all **Prices** F-FF **Rooms** 15; all with bath or shower, phone, TV **Credit cards** MC, V **Closed** end-Sept-20th Dec

Chalet hotel, Chamonix (The Alps)

Auberge du Bois Prin

A luxurious Relais & Châteaux on the north side of the Chamonix valley, this has views of the Aiguille du Midi that would have driven the 19thC Romantics crazy. Excellent food; vegetables from the garden. Informal young owners.

■ 69 Chemin de l'Hermine, Les Moussoux, 74400 Chamonix (Haute-Savoie) **Tel** 04 50 53 33 51 **Fax** 04 50 53 48 75 **Meals** all **Prices** FFF-FFFF **Rooms** 9 double; all with bath, phone, TV, minibar **Credit cards** all major **Closed** mid to end April; late Oct-early Dec

The Alps

Chalet hotel, Chamonix

Hôtel du Jeu de Paume

This newly-built pastiche of a traditional wooden chalet has mounted stags' heads, leather 'club' armchairs, pine-panelled bedrooms, four-star comfort, and is one of *the* places to stay in Chamonix. Indoor and outdoor swimming-pools.

■ 705, route du Chapeau, Le Levancher, 74400 Chamonix (Haute-Savoie) **Tel** 04 50 54 03 76 **Fax** 04 50 54 10 75 **Meals** all **Prices** FFF-FFFF **Rooms** 22; all with bath, phone, TV, heating, bar, hairdryer **Credit cards** all major **Closed** 15th May-15th Jun

Chalet hotel, Courcheval

Lodge Nogentil Hôtel

The interior of this intimate, small chalet hotel has a warm glow of polished wood and conviviality. New, young, enthusiastic owners (English, with a music-business background) had a 90 per cent fill-up rate in their first season. Chic; comfortable; very expensive.

■ 73123 Courcheval 1850 (Savoie) **Tel** 04 79 08 32 32 **Fax** 04 79 08 03 15 **Meals** breakfast **Prices** FFF-FFFF+ **Rooms** 10; all with bath, phone, sat TV, minibar, hairdryer, safe **Credit cards** all major **Closed** May and Jun

Country hotel, Doussard

Marceau Hôtel

A plain-looking, but welcoming, family-run hotel at the end of a track – ten minutes away from Lake Annecy – it has a rambling garden, dining terrace with views, and spacious bedrooms.

■ Bout du Lac, 74210 Doussard (Haute-Savoie) **Tel** 04 50 44 30 11 **Fax** 04 50 44 39 44 **Meals** all **Prices** F-FF **Rooms** 15, all with bath or shower, heating, phone, TV **Credit cards** all major **Closed** Oct-Jan

Country hotel, Echenevex

Auberge des Chasseurs

At the foot of the Jura mountains, facing the Alps, this attractive converted farmhouse is elegantly decorated and gives a warm welcome. There are beamed ceilings, and chairs and bedroom doors are painted with flowers. Pool. Reasonably priced.

■ 01170 Echenevex (Ain) **Tel** 04 50 41 54 07 **Fax** 04 50 41 90 61 **Meals** all **Prices** FF-FFF **Rooms** 15, all with bath or shower, phone, TV **Credit cards** AE, DC, MC, V **Closed** mid-Nov to mid-Mar

The Alps

Country-house hotel, Montailleur

La Tour de Pacoret

There are fine mountain views from the upper windows of this watch tower – built in the 13thC for the Dukes of Savoy and later passed to the Duc de Pacoret. It stands in a valley, surrounded by fields of corn. Informal young owners; vine-clad terrace; pretty garden.

■ Montailleur, 73460 Frontenax (Savoie) **Tel** 04 79 37 91 59 **Fax** 04 79 37 93 84 **Meals** all **Prices** F-FF **Rooms** 10; 6 with bath, 4 with shower; all with phone, TV **Credit cards** all major **Closed** 11th Nov-15th Apr

Chalet hotel, St-Gervais

Chalet Rémy

Facing Mont Blanc, this traditional stone and log chalet was a farmhouse in the 18thC and has all its original woodwork. The simple rooms are warm and have comfortable beds; Savoyard cooking.

■ Le Bettex, 74170 St-Gervais (Haute-Savoie) **Tel** 04 50 93 11 85 **Fax** 04 50 93 14 45 **Meals** all **Prices** F **Rooms** 19 double; showers and WC on landing **Credit cards** MC V **Closed** never

Ski resort hotel, Val-Thorens

Hôtel Fitz Roy

A luxurious modern chalet, with pale woodwork interior, provides an exceptionally civilized atmosphere, warm welcome, excellent Savoyard country cooking, and bedrooms with balconies and whirlpool baths.

■ 73440 Val-Thorens (Savoie) **Tel** 04 79 00 04 78 **Fax** 04 79 00 06 11 **Meals** all **Prices** FF-FFFF **Rooms** 36; all with spa bath, central heating, air-conditioning, phone, TV, minibar, hairdryer **Credit cards** all major **Closed** early May-Nov

Lakeside hotel, Veyrier-du-Lac

La Demeure de Chavoire

This impeccably-kept, charming hotel, in a pretty garden on the shores of Lake Annecy, has rooms named after famous writers – you may sleep in the Jean-Jacques Rousseau suite. Plenty of good taste and calm – on the main road to the ski resorts.

■ Route d'Annecy-Chavoire, 74290 Veyrier-du-Lac (Haute-Savoie) **Tel** 04 50 60 04 38 **Fax** 04 50 60 05 36 **Meals** breakfast, snacks **Prices** FF-FFFF **Rooms** 10, with bath, heating, phone, sat TV, minibar, hairdryer **Credit cards** all major **Closed** Sundays Jan-Dec.

Index of hotel names

In this index, hotels are arranged in order of the most distinctive part of their name; very common prefixes such as 'Auberge', 'Hôtel', 'Hostellerie' and 'La/Le/Les' are omitted, but more significant elements such as 'Château', 'Domaine' or 'Moulin' are retained.

Index of hotel names

Index of hotel names

Index of hotel locations

In this index, hotels are arranged by the name of the city, town or village they are in or near. Hotels located in a very small village may be indexed under the name of a larger place nearby.

Index of hotel locations